SHELL OSBON

Forewords by Roger Brumbalow and Wayne Elsey

IT'S NOT GOOD

FOR LEADERS

TO LEAD

ALONE!

Nobody Succeeds Without the Help of Others!

IT'S NOT GOOD
FOR LEADERS TO LEAD ALONE!

Shell Osbon

Published by:
RIGHTEOUS PEN PUBLICATIONS
(*The Righteousness of God Shall Guide My Pen*)
www.righteouspenpublications.com

DEDICATION

This book is dedicated to my father Billy Clifton Osbon, Sr. Over the course of my life, Pop taught me by example how to be a leader, regardless of position or title. Whether he was a secondary leader or a primary leader, he treated everyone he met with dignity, respect, and fairness because he knew the importance of those qualities. He also understood, at a very fundamental level, the lasting impact his words and actions had upon others.

Of all his accomplishments, I am most proud to say he served his family, his church, and his Savior with excellence. In fact, my confidence is resolute that on September 25, 2015, he heard Jesus say, "Well done, good and faithful servant; you have been faithful over a few things, I will make you ruler over many things. Enter into the joy of your Lord."

Thanks for being a leader of leaders, Pop. The world is a better place because of how you served. And when my time comes, I will know right where to find you. I love you and will see you soon.

TABLE OF CONTENTS

ACKNOWLEDGEMENTS

If you see a turtle sitting on top of a fencepost,
you know it didn't get there by itself.[1]

MANY people are familiar with the immortal "turtle on a fencepost" proverb. Truth be told, none of us can attain any significant level of success or accomplishment in life by ourselves. Somewhere along the way, others have helped us elevate from one place to the next. Their cumulative influences have made it possible for us to become who we are today. Go ahead, admit it: you did not get on that fencepost all by yourself!

For me, the list of people is extensive. It would be impossible for me name each one and to fully express my appreciation for the indelible impact they have had upon my life. Nevertheless, suffice it to say there are several people I simply cannot fail to mention, as their influence has been both life-changing and destiny-altering. These are some of the people who have helped me to climb higher than I could have on my own.

I must begin by thanking my Heavenly Father, Who was always looking for me, even when I was not looking for Him. Billy and Joyce Osbon, my parents, fervently encouraged me to pursue God's plan and provided me with every resource at their disposal to see His dream fulfilled. Missy, my devoted wife of thirty-five years, is the one through whom I receive God's favor (Proverbs 18:22). She is my perfect helpmate (Genesis 2:18). S.J. and Summer Joy, our two adult children, are incredible. I have learned more about God's love by parenting than anything else other than the Word of God. Pastor Roger Brumbalow, my spiritual father, graciously took me under his tutelage. God used him to impact my life and ministry in more ways than I can articulate.

In addition, I must express my appreciation to my dear friend Daryl Gramling for the contributions he supplied to this work. Daryl is a published author who graciously agreed to edit my writings. He also provided a wealth of insights which I have included with great delight.

After many years of stagnancy, God used Daryl to spark the fire within me and he cheered me on to the finish line. Daryl, thank you so very much!

Lastly, I would be remiss if I failed to thank the following men who helped me in different seasons of life and ministry: Dr. Bruce Wilkinson, Dr. Benson Karanja, Dr. Samuel Chand, Dr. Doug Chatham, Pastor John Palmer, Pastor Gerald Lewis, Pastor Max Phipps, Dr. M. Leonard Sapp, Pastor Phil Stephens and Dr. David Hazzard. God has used each of these wonderful men to help me become the leader that I am today, and I surely will forever be indebted to them.

FOREWORDS

WE can honestly say we are super excited to be a part of this project. When Shell first contacted us about writing a foreword in honor of our dad, it seemed like such a natural thing to do. When we began reflecting about what to write, we realized we had our work cut out for us.

I don't understand how I'm supposed to speak for my father. It's not that writing a foreword seems like an insurmountable task. My sister Claire and I struggle with the idea of stepping in for our dad. Ever since his life altering surgery in early 2008, I've been trying to fill his shoes in my own way. My dad, Roger Brumbalow, was a great man. He was a great communicator, a great leader, a good boss, and an absolute hero of a dad.

As of the writing of this book, dad is alive. He is completely disabled and dependent. Because of his condition, my sister, Claire, and I have been able to show love and loyalty to my father in ways most people may never experience. It is an honor for us to do so.

How do we put thirty-plus years into written form? Pastor Shell Osbon came into our lives in the late 1980's. I can remember showcasing my best "moonwalk attempt" for him and Missy as a preteen. I don't recall any supernatural moments in our living room during that first meeting, but something did happen between the Osbons and the Brumbalows that would impact both of our families for years to come.

My father, Roger Brumbalow, was in ministry my whole life until he was forced to retire after brain surgery left him unable to continue his work. I had seen him hire different staff. As a twelve-year-old at the time, I was excited, because Pastor Shell seemed cool and was being hired to be the youth pastor. Shell had worked for other pastors and my dad had worked with other staff...yet something was different. What formed in this hiring or transitional moment was more than a new boss/employee arrangement. A deep level relationship of loyalty and support began that day. I know that my dad sought out Shell. My dad wanted the best youth pastor in the state of Louisiana. Shell came with a good reputation, a short resume, and a lot of energy. All those things are nice, but the relationship that began to form is what truly set this pastor/staff relationship apart from any other that I've seen in my father's or Shell's life.

Dr. Mark Rutland spoke on loyalty in a Southeastern University chapel service in the early 2000's and I will never forget how he defined it: "Loyalty takes the blow and deflects the praise." I believe that is the attitude Shell Osbon embraced during the fifteen-year period in which he served my father. I believe that is the attitude with which he serves the leaders in his life, now. I can also say with confidence that I believe he extends the same loyalty to those that he leads.

Claire specifically remembered seeing this trait: there was no one ready to move faster, listen more intently and serve more whole heartedly than this man. He and Missy sat on the front row with notebook and pen, listening to every word my dad spoke. I would look over from my seat and see them writing furiously, to get every word down, so they wouldn't forget! (This was way before digital platforms and instant replays on apps and social media.)

Long story short, Roger Brumbalow is almost seventy-two years old and has been disabled/retired for thirteen years. Shell still honors him as his spiritual father today, because of that relationship. My sister and I write in our father's stead because of that relationship. Shell, Missy, and their kids became family. (Not just at our house family, but the go with us to our grandparent's house kind of family!) I recently performed the pre-marital counseling and wedding for their daughter, Summer, because of that relationship.

Shell is equipped to author this book, because it is his story. He has lived out what it means to hold up the arms of a leader, to cover the weakness of a leader, and to follow the vision of a leader.

If you are a senior or secondary leader and would like to step into a more meaningful, healthier, and more enriching relationship with your staff or leader, then you are holding the right book.

By the way, Dad gave his tearful approval to this foreword.

Rev. Keith Brumbalow and Rev. Claire Jett
(Pastor Roger Brumbalow's children)

WHEN Shell asked me to write the foreword to his book, I readily agreed to write it. Leadership is a topic that continually evolves and develops. We need as many books about leadership as we can have, so there are opportunities for everyone to understand best practices. Leadership is not a static idea, and the role models of the past need to continually get new leaders who join their ranks.

As the world emerges from the pandemic, changes that were afoot (such as flexible work schedules and remote working) have now accelerated. In short, this is a time when leadership is more necessary than ever. With apprehension and fear permeating workers because they're unsettled about their futures and how they'll provide for their families, this is an opportunity for a new kind of humanistic leader to rise.

One of the most well-worn myths is that leaders are born. No, they're not. Sure, some people might be born with the qualities that could help them become good or even great leaders, but leaders are made. In other words, they continually study leadership. They look at what other leaders do, and as they learn new ideas and ways of doing things, apply them to the work they do.

We need people who rise to the challenge of serving as leaders for their teams, communities, and the groups where they participate. It's essential that more people rise to the occasion of providing vision to others. Here, they can find motivation a path that, candidly, no one knows how it's going to unfold fully. The reality is that at a time of massive uncertainty, people need other people to share ideas and help them overcome their fears. That happens through listening, understanding, and sharing communication.

A driving theme in Shell's book is geared toward secondary leaders. Moreover, he writes about those qualities that everyone knows leaders need, but sometimes are often hard to see in people who rise up the management ladder. These are the essential qualities for good leaders who have to support the work and vision of the primary leaders.

As someone in the business world and as a global entrepreneur, the ideas that Shell writes about, in short, leaders serving others, are what I tell my team of secondary leaders to do all the time. Leaders aren't there to tell others what to do. Instead, they exist to set the vision, determine the course, and then support their teams to execute what needs to get done.

Shell's book, *It's Not Good for Leaders to Lead Alone: Nobody Succeeds Without the Help of Others*, is a message for faith-based leaders and organizations. Because of the massive disruption and changes that are now shifting our realities within short years, instead of generations, it's more vital than ever to maintain and develop our human skills.

Wayne Elsey
Founder & CEO, The Funds2Orgs Group and CEO, Elsey Enterprises

INTRODUCTION

I will come down and talk to you there. I will take some of the Spirit that is upon you, and I will put the Spirit upon them also. They will bear the burden of the people along with you, so you will not have to carry it alone.
(Numbers 11:17, NLT)

I grew up in a family with a very rich history of faithfully following Christ, but I am unaware of anyone who served in vocational ministry. As a result, I did not have the luxury of seeing full-time pastoral ministry firsthand, so as to learn how to lead a church growing up. Nevertheless, God has faithfully given me some incredible opportunities to serve others in a secondary leadership role for seventeen of the thirty-five years that I have been in ministry.

Over the course of those seventeen years, I have served four different lead pastors. One role was part-time (I worked outside the church) and the other three roles were full-time. I served in a small, rural community; a mid-sized suburban community; a medium-sized metropolitan area, and then in a major metropolitan area. I filled the diverse roles of youth pastor, business administrator, single adult pastor, and senior associate pastor during those years.

While I am grateful for the various degrees which I have earned, most of my ministry experience can best be described as on-the-job-training. There is nothing quite like trial by fire! I am thankful that God has chosen this path for me to gain these insights. I certainly have benefited from the wisdom shared by each of those four lead pastors and, as a result, I learned the principles which I will share in this book.

Admittedly, we all would prefer to learn from pleasant situations rather than from unpleasant ones. By and large, the truths I learned came from positive experiences much more so than from negative experiences. I will also acknowledge God's unique ability to teach us even during life's most difficult moments, and I believe we should learn from our trials as well as our triumphs.

The truth is that both primary and secondary leaders have huge responsibilities placed on their shoulders. Indeed, the primary leader, to a degree, may be involved in countless areas of ministry, but this writing will focus chiefly upon the roles which associate staff members maintain and upon the principles which govern secondary leadership. My goal is to share with you some of those principles. I will use Biblical examples as well as personal examples from my own experiences; however, my desire is not that this book would be "preachy," but "practical." Of course, the Word of God is practical, so I will use it often!

Relationships are the strength of any organization. If there is no real relationship between team members, then there is no cohesiveness that bonds them together when they face challenges that will certainly come their way. There is great wisdom to the adage, "no involvement, no commitment," so the development of those relationships is not only critical from a practical standpoint, but in paving the way for the organization's mission and vision to be executed.

My premise: both primary and secondary leaders should desire to have a great, dynamic relationship with each other. The success of an organization depends upon their diligent work in purposeful unity to establish, develop, and maintain those critical relationships. Just like in marriage, individual personalities and preferences will impact how those relationships develop; but there are core, underlying principles and boundaries that must be observed for the organization to function at the highest levels.

The book is laid out as a series of questions, with those questions serving as chapter headings. Each chapter focuses on a distinct aspect of servant leadership. I believe every staff member should prayerfully ask themselves these questions with a heart to effectively fulfill roles that each organization cannot function without.

Before any of this work could begin, it was abundantly necessary that I mature as a secondary leader and then become a seasoned primary leader. Having served for many years on both sides of the fence during my various ministry assignments enables me to share principles that collectively make churches and organizations more effective. A recurring theme will be scriptures reminding that we are part of one body. In keeping with those truths, there certainly is no intention in assigning relative values to "secondary" or "primary" leaders, nor are the principles intended to be self-serving for those in primary roles. In fact, my overarching goal, both as a lead pastor and in this book, is to enable those who serve in secondary roles to become more effective. The best leaders are not those who can somehow control others, but the ones who can encourage and inspire others to reach new heights and become all they were intended to be.

To that end, I believe this book will not only be useful within the church; its principles are also applicable outside church. Wherever there are leaders, this book's principles can be applied. The reality is an organization will only reach its maximum potential as the entire leadership team becomes stronger – including both the primary leader and those in secondary leadership roles.

Some will recognize the title of this work, *It's Not Good for Leaders to Lead Alone!* to be inspired by Genesis 2:18. In the earliest days of human history (back in the Garden of Eden), God declared: *It is not good that man should be alone; I will make a helper comparable to him.*

Similarly, I am convinced no leader should ever have to lead an organization alone. Just as God knew man needed a suitable helper, each primary leader needs a staff of talented, wise, and effective secondary leaders to help bring the vision to pass. We have been created to share life together and to achieve for God's kingdom what none of us could ever hope to do alone. It is not for personal glory, but that in everything we do, we do it for the glory of God.

> Relationships are the strength of any organization. If there is no real relationship between team members, then there is no cohesiveness that bonds them together when they face challenges that will certainly come their way.

Former Vice Chairman and Principal Creative Executive at Walt Disney Imagineering Martin Sklar once said:

> "Some of the biggest talents I have worked with - designers, writers, sculptors, architects and many more - loved those blank pages, but had no interest in the responsibility of team building. You can be a lone ranger and a star at golf, tennis or a 20k run, but the only name on the door around our company is Walt Disney. We play the ultimate team game."[1]

It is for this essential purpose that I humbly present to you, *It's Not Good for Leaders to Lead Alone!* May your leadership capacity – whether primary or secondary – continue to develop and be strengthened as you study and then apply these timeless truths from the

Greatest Book ever written!

CHAPTER 1

AN OLYMPIC-SIZED LESSON IN LEADERSHIP

*Don't you realize that in a race everyone runs, but only one person gets
the prize? So run to win! All athletes are disciplined in their training.
They do it to win a prize that will fade away, but we do it for an eternal prize.*
(1 Corinthians 9:24-25, NLT)

ONE of the great things about watching the Olympics is hearing the most incredible stories of how an unknown athlete overcame seemingly impossible odds. Sometimes we also discover the back story behind the unlikely individuals whose passion and commitment helped write the athlete's story. Perhaps one of the greatest examples is found in the poignant story of Derek Redmond. Derek was a British athlete who, at one point, held the British record for the 400-meter sprint. He was no stranger to world championships and with multiple gold medals to his name, it would seem a tall order to find someone who could hold a candle to his remarkable achievements. Even Visa and Nike ran advertisements featuring videos of him running on the track at the Barcelona Olympics in 1992.

But wait.

Behind every great athlete is at least one great coach, supporter, mentor, or cheerleader. If ever that statement was true, it shone brightly on that track in Spain. Derek's time in the first round of competition was the fastest. In short order, he won the quarter final, as well. But his fortune turned during the semi-final, when he abruptly tore his hamstring and collapsed onto the track in abject pain. Now imagine, if you will, just how much pain that would cause someone. Forget the hamstring; we are talking about someone who has spent most of his life training for this event. We are talking about an athlete so focused on winning the Gold that it guided virtually every decision he made in his entire adult life.

He was not a thirteen-year-old boy, a thousand miles away on a dusty track with torn sneakers with a slim chance of making it as an athlete. He is on the track, on worldwide television, with the finish line and a gold medal in plain sight. Every fiber of his spirit screams out, "No! No, this cannot be happening! Not here, not now!" But it did happen. The finish line may as well have been on the moon. It was over.

But wait.

The cameras picked up some guy dashing past the security team on the track. Something he said to them must have carried weight, as they let him proceed toward Derek, who still wanted to finish the course. But how to move another inch with a torn hamstring? The answer came and history was made as Jim Redmond, Derek's father, ran to him and slid an arm around him. Together, they hobbled down the remaining stretch of track to cross the finish line. Sixty-five thousand fans stood in genuine honor, if not awe, to give them both a standing ovation. It became one of the finest moments in modern Olympics.

> What this book is about, and what you need to understand in your spirit, is the incredible value of the individuals who make it happen for others.

This book is about the Jim Redmonds of the world. I have no idea if the senior Mr. Redmond could have run a mile to save his own life, but without him setting foot on the track on that fateful day, the 1992 Olympics would have been far less memorable. Medals would still have been handed out, but it just would not have been the same, and countless lives would not have been touched in the many years since as the video chronicling this epic and most wonderful turn of events continues to be shared.

What this book is about, and what you need to understand in your spirit, is the incredible value of the individuals who make it happen for others. Take any success story you want, and you'll find an English teacher who inspired some kid to write his first short story. Twenty years later, that kid releases a best-selling novel and thanks the teacher who made it possible. Then there's the very young girl with such poor self-esteem, she cannot bear to see her own reflection in a mirror. Still, her Sunday School teacher tells her how beautiful she is. Fifteen years later, her wonderful and utterly breathtaking smile graces the cover of a major magazine.

Then there's the senior pastor of a church of any size. They've been kicked, punched, and embattled in every conceivable way, rarely more than spitting distance from giving up and quitting amid the most recent set of difficult circumstances (such are common in ministry). There was a secondary leader – a youth minister perhaps, or the church secretary. Maybe it was a parking lot attendant or the guy that runs the sound booth every other Wednesday night. They may not even have a formal title, but when they saw their leader down, they pushed through security, ran to him without regard to the screaming crowd, and slipped their arm around him to help him up. With countless voices in heaven cheering them on in thunderous applause, this servant leader pushes past the finish line.

If you are in secondary leadership, this book is all about you. Most of the work in every organization is done behind the scenes, with no cameras, no spotlights, and moments of personal glory, usually few and far between. We must remember the world's system of rewards has it all backwards; God is able to reward us for what we do. As we find from the inspiring story of Jim Redmond, it is a reminder the organization where you serve could not do it without you.

Should you wonder if being a secondary leader matters, think of these famous duos and ask yourself what the world would be like with only the first person:

- Abbott and Costello
- Batman and Robin
- Baskin and Robbins
- Scooby Doo and Shaggy
- Tom and Jerry
- Woody and Buzz Lightyear
- Yogi and Boo Boo
- Starsky and Hutch
- Mickey Mouse and Minnie Mouse
- Laurel and Hardy
- Cheech and Chong
- Andy Griffith and Barney Fife
- Kermit the Frog and Miss Piggy
- Michael Jordan and Scottie Pippen
- Skipper and Gilligan
- Simon and Garfunkel
- Fred Astaire and Ginger Rogers
- Sherlock Holmes and Watson
- Fred Flintstone and Barney Rubble

> Most of the work in every organization is done behind the scenes, with no cameras, no spotlights, and moments of personal glory, usually few and far between.

- Tom Sawyer and Huckleberry Finn
- Captain Kirk and Spock
- The Lone Ranger and Tonto
- Elijah and Elisha
- Moses and Aaron
- Paul and Silas

Make no mistake about it – you are making history. Just as Vince Lombardi once said:

"The man on top of the mountain didn't fall there."[1]

- **Reflect:** Which characteristics or qualities exemplify your leadership, whether you are a primary leader or secondary leader?

- **Receive:** Mark 9:35: *Jesus says, "Whoever wants to be first must take last place and be the servant of everyone else."*

- **Respond:** Name at least two things you can do better to exemplify the type of leadership Jesus says His followers should model.

MY REFLECTIONS

CHAPTER 2

WHAT IS A SECONDARY LEADER?

Don't think only about your own affairs,
but be interested in others, too, and what they are doing.
(Philippians 2:4, NLT)

BEING "at the top" of the organizational chart is not a mandate to part ways with humility. Instead, it is an opportunity to demonstrate servant leadership by personal example and instill that crucial trait throughout the organization. It is important that staff members do not define themselves or the value of their roles in terms of where they are on the totem pole. It is, rather, their purpose to focus on how effectively they can do the role which God has assigned to them.

In Matthew 25:16-18 we read a story Jesus told, which supports this truth: *Again, the Kingdom of Heaven can be illustrated by the story of a man going on a long trip. He called together his servants and entrusted his money to them while he was gone. He gave five bags of silver to one, two bags of silver to another, and one bag of silver to the last - dividing it in proportion to their abilities. He then left on his trip. The servant who received the five bags of silver began to invest the money and earned five more. The servant with two bags of silver also went to work and earned two more. But the servant who received the one bag of silver dug a hole in the ground and hid the master's money."* (NLT, emphasis added)

The parable of the talents reinforces the reality that everyone has a different leadership capacity. The ones with fewer talents were not in any way disregarded based upon the number of talents placed in their hands. The emphasis is the call to set aside our own desires, so the vision of the organization is achieved. God will honor our support of this leader, and likewise will dishonor selfishly ambitious attempts to subvert that vision and replace it with our own.

It is also worth noting that the same God who has the plan for the senior leader also has an equally important plan for each secondary leader. The body is not divided; the hand and foot cannot compete to say which is more important. Secondary leadership is often the launching board from which youth pastors are given the opportunity to become associate pastors, or from which associate pastors are offered the position of senior pastor.

> Remain faithful in what you do, year after year.

Additionally, whereas secondary leaders may, in a sense, be asked to surrender their identity, sometimes God will elevate the secondary leader far beyond their imagination. Joseph was a servant in the home of an Egyptian captain named Potiphar. Potiphar evidently had great wealth, because we are told he kept entrusting more and more to Joseph. Nowhere do we read Joseph had his eye on owning a thing belonging to Potiphar. In the end, who do we know about? Who was the mover and shaker in the Old Testament, Potiphar or Joseph?

Remain faithful in what you do, year after year. Don't worry if you have plaques on your walls commemorating how much the senior leader appreciates you or how much the church at large has publicly applauded your achievements thus far. Do not waste time longing to have the corner office with windows on the top floor of your office building. Work diligently with a servant's heart. If God wishes to elevate you to a different position, then He will do so. Doors will open and you will be able to walk through them with head held high, knowing it is God Who is opening that door for you and ushering you through it rather than anything which might even have a whiff of selfish ambition. In truth, when God elevates you, everyone else will know it, and they will not be able to do a thing to hold you back.

> Organizations need primary leaders and secondary leaders.
>
> Primary leaders need secondary leaders.
>
> Secondary leaders need primary leaders.
>
> We all need each other, because nobody succeeds without the help of others.

For the sake of clarity, I want to stress that "primary leader" and "secondary leaders" are mutually essential roles to the success of any organization. Neither the terms, nor the respective definitions, imply the value of a position, but rather what God's heart is for each. A common theme throughout this book will be we are all parts of one body. There can never be the notion that the left arm is somehow more important than the right leg.

A soccer team has the offensive positions of left, center, and right forwards, designed primarily to score goals. The guy who kicks best with his left leg needs to be on the left side, not because he is a better forward than the guy on the right side of the field, but because it is where the player's natural skills lie. The defenders that stay far behind the forwards do not have a lesser role. They support the forwards by getting the ball to them to position them to score. If they cannot defend their team's goal effectively, it does not matter how many goals the forwards score; they still will lose.

The same is true within every church and organization. Everyone cannot be the Lead Pastor, nor the CEO. Those are roles occupied by one person for a particular period. On the other hand, every church and every business must be staffed with essentially important secondary leaders. In fact, while the primary leaders provide the overall vision, it will be the secondary leaders who fulfill the necessary tasks which move the organization forward.

1 Corinthians 12:14-21 reminds us: *The human body has many parts, but the many parts make up one whole body. So, it is with the body of Christ. Yes, the body has many different parts, not just one part. If the foot says, 'I am not a part of the body because I am not a hand,' that does not make it any less a part of the body. And if the ear says, 'I am not part of the body because I am not an eye,' would that make it any less a part of the body? If the whole body were an eye, how would you hear? Or if your whole body were an ear, how would you smell anything? But our bodies have many parts, and God has put each part just where he wants it. How strange a body would be if it had only one part! Yes, there are many parts, but only one body. The eye can never say to the hand, 'I don't need you.' The head can't say to the feet, 'I don't need you.* (NLT)

Organizations need primary leaders and secondary leaders.

Primary leaders need secondary leaders.

Secondary leaders need primary leaders.

We all need each other, because nobody succeeds without the help of others.

- **Reflect:** How many effective primary leaders would you say learned how to lead by first being secondary leaders?

- **Receive:** Matthew 20:25-26a: *But Jesus called them together and said, "You know that the rulers in this world lord it over their people, and officials flaunt their authority over those under them. But among you it will be different."* (NLT)

- **Respond:** List three things you can do better in your current role.

MY REFLECTIONS

CHAPTER 3

DO YOU HELP CARRY YOUR LEADER'S LOAD?

Bear one another's burdens, and so fulfill the law of Christ.
(Galatians 6:2)

OVER the years I have served as a lead pastor, I have heard a few comments by staff members who felt they were carrying a heavier load than the one that I was carrying. Sometimes the comments were rather subtle, such as, "I really wish I could spend more time with my family" or "I just don't have very much free time." Those things are usually said when the person is trying to let you know they have been working hard and believe they deserve time off. They might also be said to convince you they work at least as hard, if not harder, than you.

I can still remember one memorable occasion when a staff member, as I was addressing his chronic tardiness, abandoned all subtlety and said, "I noticed you aren't always here when the office opens each day." Wait, what did he just say? Are you kidding me? I need to tell you that I was shocked by his arrogance and really could not believe he would say that. It was almost as if he believed his schedule was equal to mine or that his load was the same as mine and neither could be further from the truth. As a result, I placed him on a ninety-day probationary period, hoping he would realize the error of his ways. Sadly, that staff member did not stay with me much longer and never seemed to learn his lesson.

To be sure, I am a strong believer in the importance of quality family time. I also am a firm believer a church staff should have a strong work ethic. In this case, the problem was not the staff member's sincere desire to spend time with his family. It is vitally important that staff members invest in their own families and make time for relaxation. The problem was a staffer's unfortunate arrogance in presuming that his schedule was equal to mine. Whether or not it was obvious to the staffer, the truth is that he had it mighty easy in comparison to the never-ending pressures borne by senior leadership.

Sometimes a staff member can think the load they carry is greater than the load the primary leader carries. Consider for example how many times a casual visitor to our church may have observed the service. As the service concludes and he prepares to head to The Golden Corral for lunch, he quips to his wife, "It must be nice to be the senior pastor of a church – all you have to do is preach for an hour each week and you're done. You know what, I bet somebody even cuts his grass for him!" To the uninitiated, it is quite easy to vastly underestimate the amount of sermon preparation, staff meetings, leadership efforts, mentoring activities, community relationship building, budget planning, personnel issues, weddings, funerals, maintenance issues, long-term development, and countless other necessary claims on a pastor's time. From there, it then becomes easy to even resent how good the leader must have it! If only the pastor had to deal with all the issues of the church office! If only he knew how hard it was to build a youth department in an immoral world! Having served in associate pastoral roles for seventeen years and now having served as a lead pastor for the past eighteen years, I can unequivocally state that the primary leader's load is *much* heavier than any load I ever carried as an associate pastor or in any other role, for that matter. It does not compare.

> No other person on the team carries a load that even comes close to that which the primary leader must carry.

While it may sometimes be true that a staff member works more hours on site than the primary leader and while it is even possible that they may know more about some areas of the organization, the reality is that no other person on the team carries a load that even comes close to that which the primary leader must carry. In fact, everything that goes wrong may not be the primary leader's fault, but everything is still his or her responsibility in some shape or form. This truth can be quite easily confirmed by asking anyone on the street who gets the blame if a church is struggling. No one would suggest the youth pastor needs to get his or her act together, and few would opine that the worship leader needs to find some new songs. All heads invariably turn to the senior leadership and wonder aloud why the primary leader hasn't fixed whatever the problem may be.

The essence of this reality can be seen in an examination of the events in the Garden of Gethsemane as Jesus approached the hour of His crucifixion. Matthew chapter 26 records that while He was in deep, agonizing prayer – literally to the point of sweating drops of blood – the disciples were fast asleep. Jesus was literally pouring out His heart because of the weight He was carrying as the disciples rested peacefully in the garden.

I have discovered in my more than thirty-five years of ministry experience that there is rarely a moment when the lead pastor's mind is free from thinking about someone in church who is going through a difficult time. There is always a family whose teenage daughter is struggling with her sexuality, a single mom whose young adult son has become addicted to alcohol, a couple whose marriage of twenty-five years seems to be on the verge of ending in a bitter divorce, the family who has become infrequent in their attendance and who appears to be leaving the church. The painful list goes on and on and on and on. While associate staff members do indeed have their own load to carry, it will never compare to the weight carried by the lead pastor. From a confidentiality standpoint alone, there are countless burdens placed on senior leaders that no one else can be aware of, much less carry.

There is a member of our church who is a department-level technology manager at his employer's company, himself a secondary leader in every respect. He puts in many long hours, and on occasion has been so utterly exhausted after a grueling six-day workweek that he did not even make it to church on Sunday. He was reduced by sheer exhaustion to catching a sermon online. Look at what he has to say about the nature of secondary leadership:

> "The truth is that I am often overwhelmed at the amount of work that must be done within our department, and if my own staffers are not able to complete the job, then I expect it of myself to get my hands dirty and figure out a solution, even if that means working evenings or weekends. It is not uncommon for me to work longer than my boss and to lock up the building hours after everyone else has gone home for the day. That's not fair, right? But then I consider just how hard the owners must work. They may or may not be in the office putting in visibly impressive hours, but over the years of working for them, I have witnessed just how much they care about each of their employees. I have seen them make excruciating decisions during leaner times so that the rank-and-file employees could have a Christmas bonus, even if

they had to forgo their own bonus. I have personally set them up with remote desktop capabilities, which means they can extend their hours from home, securely accessing the company's resources from home or even while on vacation. Their jobs are never done and in the weekly management meetings a mind-boggling array of issues are constantly being brought up and addressed that I have no responsibility for.

"In all honesty, I then compare their load to mine, and realize that numerically speaking, I have a small department of just a few people, whereas they are responsible for all employees in the entire company. I have a hundred things on my plate; they have a hundred plates. When I gave enough consideration to this truth, it made it a lot easier to accept the reality that they have vastly higher levels of responsibility than I. My job, therefore, is to wisely use the resources with which I have been entrusted, and to marshal those resources to support the greater goals of the company. Maybe I agree with the senior leadership on a given point and maybe I don't; but if I don't, I nonetheless have the sure knowledge that I don't see everything they see. Truly, their levels of responsibility greatly eclipse my own."

On that note, Carey Nieuwhof asserts one of the best ways that a secondary leader can effectively implement change is to think like a senior leader. More specifically, Carey says:

"Imagine the pressures and issues facing your senior leader and approach the conversation accordingly. Think through how it impacts the entire organization. Showing your senior leader, you understand the bigger picture is huge."[1]

> There is rarely a moment when the lead pastor's mind is free from thinking about someone in church who is going through a difficult time.

2 Samuel chapter 3 records for us how Saul's son, Abner, defected

and aligned himself with David to fight against his father's army. The story continues with how Joab, one of David's officers, killed Abner believing he would betray David. Although this was done without his knowledge and while he was not personally at fault for Abner's death, David mourned, because he knew he had a level of responsibility for everything that happened under his leadership. In some shape or form, these types of burdens weigh heavily and exact a heavy toll on the leader.

Exodus chapter 39 contains another great example of this principle. God gave instructions to Moses on how to build the tent of meeting, including furnishings and utensils. The extraordinarily elaborate details for each item would have been overwhelming for Moses to monitor and maintain. Thankfully, he was not alone in the work. Verse 42 states, *According to all that the Lord had commanded Moses, so the children of Israel did all the work.* Moses' job was to receive the vision from God and share it with the people. From that point, their role was to do the work so that the godly vision would be fulfilled. If we try to put ourselves in Moses' shoes for a moment, we would not think God wanted one lone individual to singlehandedly build everything, would we? Indeed, the reason some primary leaders fail is they are expected to take on far too much of the load that is better borne by the organization.

> Although staff members may see a portion of the vision, it remains the duty of the primary leader to see the greater vision and know what must take place to achieve the vision of the organization.

Ephesians 4:11-12 reminds us, *Christ is the One Who gave these gifts to the church: the apostles, the prophets, the evangelists, and the pastors and teachers. Their responsibility is to equip God's people to do His work and build up the church, the body of Christ.* (CEV) It is apparent from these verses that the purpose of ecclesiastical leadership is to train others to serve in the work of the church, rather than the pastor trying to do the work alone.

1 Corinthians chapter 12 reinforces the perspective that the body is comprised of many parts, but that every part is important for the overall purposes of the Body. More specifically, verse 12 states, *The body of Christ has many different parts, just as any other body does.* (CEV) It is not just a matter of many hands lightening the workload. As a local body of believers, we thrive when we work together in unity and with a common

purpose. A tedious job is made much more enjoyable, or at least much less mundane, when others join in with us. There is strength in unity; there is joy in commonality.

Mark chapter 14 records how the disciples helped Jesus in the miracle of the fish and loaves by distributing (sowing) and gathering (reaping). Jesus had the vision and the strategy, but the disciples did the work required for the task. This is a classic example of how a leader should not lead alone. Even Jesus needed help!

In Numbers chapter 11, the Israelites complained bitterly because they did not have their preferred foods. Stressed by their foul attitudes and the sheer weight of leading over two million people, Moses told God to kill him if that is the way things were going to be. Fortunately, God did not choose to respond to Moses' perspective. Instead, He responded to Moses' need. Numbers 11:17 shows that God assigned seventy leaders to Moses so that ...*they'll then be able to take some of the load of this people - you won't have to carry the whole thing alone.* (MSG) It is perfectly scriptural to understand that in any organization, the primary leader should not lead alone. Secondary leaders must come alongside, sharing in both the difficult work and the lasting joy of seeing God's purposes unfold.

As in the earlier years of His life, Jesus continued to need help in carrying His load, even in the last hours of His life. Recall that after being mercilessly beaten and severely flogged, the soldiers then demanded Jesus carry this instrument of death alone (a customary part of the punishment associated with crucifixion). Interestingly, Matthew 27:32 records the journey to Golgotha by saying, *Along the way, they came across a man named Simon, who was from Cyrene, and the soldiers forced him to carry Jesus' cross.* (NLT) Was Simon dimly qualified to die in Jesus' place? Certainly not. Could he remotely have carried Jesus' full load? Obviously not. By hoisting that heavy burden onto his shoulders and fearfully trudging ahead through the crowded streets, he successfully fulfilled a necessary role, even in the middle of horrific circumstances. Here, he became part of history. Wherever this full account of Jesus' trials is told, Simon's name and contribution are mentioned.

Thankfully, there are no legions of cruel soldiers, screaming commands in the middle of our church offices these days. Indeed, staff members have been called by God to help their primary leader facilitate the miracle of ministry and multiplication. Each one has an assigned role within their organization, which they are uniquely called to fill. Although staff members may see a portion of the vision, it remains the duty of the primary leader to see the greater vision and know what must take place to achieve the vision of the organization.

> "Lonely and alone, discouraged and empty hearted, that's when a man needs a brother. When the burden is heavy, the load too much to bear, that's when a man needs a brother. When in despair, and needing someone to care, that's when a man needs a brother. When the words, 'we'll make it through together' seem so sweet, that's when a man needs a brother. When courage is needed and strength to carry on, that's when a man needs a brother. When you think you can do it alone, that's when a man needs a brother."[2]

Carey Nieuwhof says:

> "If you're discontent...it's not that difficult to drift into the category of critic. Unless – that is – you decide to be part of the solution. Offer help. Don't end-run your leader, run with your leader on the project. Be the most helpful you can be. Offer to do the leg work. Bring your best ideas to the table every day. Offer to help in any way you can. If you won't be part of the solution, you'll eventually become part of the problem."[3]

In his book *Who's Holding Your Ladder?*, my friend, Dr. Samuel Chand poignantly writes,

> "Nobody ever climbed Mt. Everest without a team. No matter how high we go we should be holding somebody else's ladder - that's God's plan. As leaders, when we start upward, our most important decision is to choose the right ladder holders; as ladder holders, our most important decision is to select which ladders we hold. When we accomplish great things on our own ladder, we remember what we've done. When we intentionally hold others' ladders and they accomplish great things, they remember us. Their achievements become our legacy."[4]

Although everything that goes wrong may not be his or her fault or even within their control, make it a point to help your leader carry the weight of whatever happens on their watch. The truth is that, at times, the weight is virtually unbearable!

- **Reflect:** Is there anything which keeps you from carrying the load your leader needs you to carry?

- **Receive:** Galatians 6:2: *You obey the law of Christ when you offer each other a helping hand.* (CEV)

- **Respond:** Consider talking to your leader, acknowledging you may not fully know or be able to appreciate the load he carries. If there is any area which you feel you have not carried your load as you should, acknowledge this and identify steps you will take to serve more effectively.

MY REFLECTIONS

CHAPTER 4

DO YOU HAVE CONFIDENCE IN YOUR LEADER?

But the other men who had explored the land with him disagreed.
"We can't go up against them! They are stronger than we are!"
So they spread this bad report about the land among the Israelites:
"The land we traveled through and explored will devour anyone who goes
to live there. All the people we saw were huge. We even saw giants there,
the descendants of Anak. Next to them we felt like grasshoppers,
and that's what they thought, too!"
(Numbers 13:31-33, NLT)

CONFIDENCE can be defined as the belief you can have faith in or rely on someone. There are countless qualities a primary leader must possess. These range from integrity, leadership skills, preaching and teaching ability, a strong work ethic, interpersonal skills, and many more. None of these qualities will be of much value if the secondary leaders do not have confidence in the leader's ability to lead the organization.

Moses sent twelve spies into the Promised Land with specific instructions as to what they were to do. He provided them with job descriptions articulating what was expected of them. (It is worth pointing out that these spies might be considered secondary leaders!) All twelve spies performed their assigned duties, as none were negligent in doing exactly what they were told to do. The problem came, however, not in the performance of tasks, but in the confidence they placed in their leader, Moses.

All twelve spies saw the same things and did the same things. They each accepted their mission, faithfully checked out the land and its inhabitants, and returned to report to Moses. Unfortunately, ten spies were not willing to have confidence in what God called Moses to do. Nevertheless, Joshua and Caleb had confidence in Moses, as noted in Numbers 14:6-8: *But Joshua the son of Nun and Caleb...who were among*

> Joshua and Caleb were able to put their firm confidence in Moses because they recognized he was faithfully following God.

those who had spied out the land, tore their clothes; and they spoke to all the congregation of the children of Israel, saying: 'The land we passed through to spy out is an exceedingly good land. If the Lord delights in us, then He will bring us into this land and give it to us, a land which flows with milk and honey.'

Joshua and Caleb were able to put their firm confidence in Moses because they recognized he was faithfully following God. Had Moses been unfaithful to God, they would not have placed much confidence in his ability to lead God's people to their appointed destiny. Because they could see God's hand upon his life, they were able to stand behind him and support the God-given vision to the best of their abilities.

Another classic example of how a leader is positively affected by the confidence placed in him can be seen in 1 Samuel chapter 14. In this story, Jonathan and his armor bearer were secretly planning to attack the Philistines (the archenemies of the Israelites). As Jonathan is contemplating what they should do, we read in verses 6 and 7: *Then Jonathan said to the young man who bore his armor, 'Come, let us go over to the garrison of these uncircumcised; it may be that the Lord will work for us. For nothing restrains the Lord from saving by many or by few.' So his armor bearer said to him, 'Do all that is in your heart. Go then; here I am with you, according to your heart.'*

Place yourself in the position of the primary leader. If you had been Jonathan, what would it mean to you for those around you to express their solidarity toward you and confidence in your leadership? Conversely, imagine the deep disappointment of hearing a second-hand conversation in which the armor bearer expressed dissatisfaction or even contempt for his leader? Indeed, well-placed confidence in the leader can serve to strengthen him or her during the most difficult of times. Never pass up an opportunity to do that. It is worth noting the armor bearer would not know everything Jonathan knew, and he didn't even have to agree with Jonathan on every single point. What was important is he expressed resolute confidence in Jonathan's ability to achieve what God had, in fact, placed on his heart.

In 2 Samuel chapter 7, Nathan is summoned to King David. He learns the king wants to build a tabernacle in which the Lord's presence will reside: *Now it came to pass when the king was dwelling in his house, and the Lord had given him rest from all his enemies all around, that the king said to Nathan the prophet, 'See now, I dwell in a house of cedar, but the ark of God dwells inside tent curtains.' Then Nathan said to the king, "Go, do all that is in your heart, for the Lord is with you."* In this particular case, God would not allow David to build the tabernacle. He did grant his son, Solomon, that privilege, which was only possible through the support David provided prior to his death.

The phrase *"...do that all that is in your heart..."* is what every primary leader longs to hear from their staff. Of course, the caveat to this carte blanche support is that the staff needs to have the assurance their leader's heart is moving in the right direction for the best results.

Carey Nieuwhof aptly writes:

> "If your staff team, elder board or other leaders around you have lost confidence in you for more than a season, it's time to go. It means your influence as a leader is gone, and without the ability to influence, you can't lead."[1]

Unless the primary leader is unfaithful, ungodly or unethical, every associate leader should be able to have confidence in his or her leadership ability.

While this is true of others' confidence in you, it is also true of your confidence in your primary leader.

There are some staff members who have enough confidence to join their leader partway on a trek through the wilderness, but lack the confidence it takes to see it through to fruition and enter the Promised Land. If you have insufficient confidence in your primary leader, you will never be able to fully possess the place God has destined for your church or organization.

Sam Rainer once wrote:

> "The best followers are loyal. They don't let insignificant mistakes by the leader cloud their overall perception. They understand the leader's foibles and accept them. They simply look for a general trend of sound decisions and stick with their leader."[2]

Mike Bonem expounds on the importance of having confidence in your primary leader by saying:

> "Effectiveness in the second chair, more than any other role,

depends on a great relationship with the first chair leader. A high level of trust, an ability to use complementary gifts without feeling threatened, and collaboration on direction-setting decisions are clear signs that you are doing your job well."[3]

That is great wisdom indeed.

Unless the primary leader is unfaithful, ungodly or unethical, every associate leader should be able to have confidence in his or her leadership ability. There will certainly be times when their decisions may not be the same as you would make. Their style of leadership may be different than yours. Regardless, having confidence is paramount to having a healthy relationship with them and to the health of the organization where you serve.

- **Reflect:** How much confidence do you have in your leader?

- **Receive:** Proverbs 14:28: *The mark of a good leader is loyal followers; leadership is nothing without a following.* (The Message).

- **Respond:** Prayerfully consider how you can better express your confidence in your primary leader and develop greater loyalty to his/her leadership.

MY REFLECTIONS

CHAPTER 5

DO YOU SUPPORT YOUR LEADER'S VISION?

Lord, open his eyes that he may see.
(2 Kings 17:6)

THE English word "vision" comes from the Latin word *videre* which means, "to see." In light of this chapter's focus, my concern is not about your physical vision, but if you are able to embrace the vision God has given to your primary leader. If a leader's vision is not apparent to and supported by the secondary leaders, the vision will never be fully attained. The primary leader cannot do it all; such a scenario is mathematically, physically, and spiritually impossible. That is why God has placed you in your role. It is why God has gifted you with unique ability, insight, ideas, and creativity. He had no intention for the primary leader to shoulder the full weight of the organization. He certainly had no intention for the primary leader to receive all the rewards for a job well done. Do not miss out on those rewards, even if the journey entails lots of very hard work.

Within the scope of church ministry, there may be no single issue as potentially divisive as when a staff member struggles with trying to fulfill his vision versus fulfilling the pastor's vision. This rarely happens all at once, but occurs over a period of time in which a staff member begins questioning small decisions. Maybe the office hours are too long or could be more flexible. Maybe vacation policies should be tweaked. Did we really need to paint the halls that horrid color? These may seem rather minor in the grand scheme of things, but they sometimes escalate to the point where every decision is questioned. When that happens, division and confusion are aggressively lurking just around the corner. That is precisely what our enemy wants.

Regrettably, far too many of us in church have witnessed firsthand the damage and fallout when this takes place. Regardless of a person's intentions, God is never glorified when division takes place in the local church as the result of a staff member's divisiveness. Churches are damaged. People's confidence in their spiritual leaders is undermined. Far worse, the enemy of our souls is absolutely thrilled when the church of Jesus Christ becomes fragmented over multiple visions. We know from John 10:10 the enemy comes to kill, steal, and destroy. Divisions offer fertile ground for the enemy to sow deadly seeds of destruction. When such division happens within the church itself, what a win it is for the enemy!

When the lead pastor and a staff member have two different visions, what they have is "di−vision." Division is defined as "a partition that divides two groups or things." When division exists, the stability of the church and its effectiveness are jeopardized. In fact, 1 Corinthians 12:24-25 states, *God has tempered the body together...that there might be no division in the body, but that the members might have the same concern one for another.* (DARBY)

> There will be times when the leader is the only one that may "see" what God is doing in a particular situation.

While that is true, please do not presume that division only occurs within ministry. On the contrary, leaders within every segment of society must be on guard. If not, their organization can just as easily fall prey to this demon of division. To that point, Brad Waggoner states:

> "Work hard to stay aligned with the leadership in your organization."[1]

The operative words in that sentence are "work hard," because it certainly will not be easy. Creating division is relatively easy; maintaining strong unity takes work.

In 2 Kings chapter 6, we see a classic example of this principle. This is the story of when Elisha and his servant were surrounded by the Syrian armies. Upon seeing the immense army, Elisha's dear servant rather understandably became overwhelmed! He came to Elisha in a blind panic and asked what in the world they were going to do. Elisha very calmly responded that those who were with them were more numerous than those who were against them. Please observe the quiet, confident vision this primary leader projected. It gets so much better, teaching us a very powerful lesson in primary leadership. In verse 17, we read how Elisha prayed: *"'Lord, open his eyes that he may see.' Then the Lord opened the eyes of the young man and he saw the mountain was full of horses and chariots of fire all around Elisha."*

There will be times when the leader is the only one that may "see" what God is doing in a particular situation. At that moment, it becomes the responsibility of staff members to support the pastor's vision, even when they don't see it like he sees it! The primary responsibility for "seeing" where God is leading the church will always rest upon the shoulders of the lead pastor. Others may be able to recognize it, but God always flows through His established order of authority in the local church.

In support of this reality, Mike Bonem poignantly says:

> "Vision alignment. There is a difference between someone with great ideas and passion, and someone with their own vision. In the latter case, the rest of the organization is sure to end up confused about which vision is really being pursued."[2]

It is of enormous importance to prayerfully align with the leader's vision. It is utterly critical to pray that the Holy Spirit will illuminate in greater measure whatever direction and resources are needed for God's kingdom to advance within the local church.

Jesus says, in Matthew 12:25: *Every kingdom, city or house divided against itself will not stand.* Note that Jesus made this declaration on the heels of being accused of casting out demons by the power of Satan. In verse 26, Christ went on to say: *If Satan casts out Satan, he is divided against himself. How then will his kingdom stand?* God is not the author of confusion. Conflicting visions for the same body of believers do not advance the kingdom.

Although it may not necessarily be demonic in and of itself, multiple visions do have a way of leading to deep problems. Indeed, part of the primary leader's job is to marshal a variety of

> When staff members firmly support the God-given vision of the lead pastor and as unity prevails in the church, the anointing will flow, the Water of Life, Jesus Christ, will cause everything to flourish.

"good" ideas, goals, and activities to bring people together under a common vision. It certainly is unlikely that every lead pastor and staff member will always see eye to eye, and great leaders are prudent to not only hear, but even embrace different ways of accomplishing the ultimate goals. The fact that God gave the senior pastor a strategic vision of the next generation of ministry hardly precludes the pastor from incorporating many tactical and operational ideas from a variety of qualified sources within the organization to accomplish that vision. The Biblical mandate is not to be identical. The Biblical mandate is to be unified.

In Exodus chapter 32, while Moses was on the mountain top receiving the Ten Commandments from God, Aaron was in the valley, responding to the demands of the Israelites. As a result of his inability to understand and support the vision that God gave to Moses, Aaron gave the people what they wanted (a golden calf to worship). This was in contrast to what God desired them to have (a moral code by which to live). The immediate result was God sent a plague upon the people to punish their idolatry. The long-term result was that the Israelites were forced to choose between two different leaders with two different visions.

David writes of the importance of unity in Psalm 133:1-3: *Behold, how good and how pleasant it is for brethren to dwell together in unity! It is like the precious oil upon the head, running down the beard, the beard of Aaron, running down on the edge of his garments. It is like the dew of Hermon descending upon the mountains of Zion; For there the Lord commanded the blessing - life forevermore.* The unity David speaks of is compared to anointing oil, which was placed upon Aaron, as the high priest.

As a practical matter, when we anoint someone with oil in a church service, we typically use a tiny amount. During altar ministry, we are careful to use the smallest amount possible so as not to get any on the recipient's clothing. Aaron's anointing included several gallons of very aromatic oil so he would literally be drenched as it ran from his head down to his toes! That is a vivid picture of how God wants unity to work – He literally desires that unity prevail from top to bottom within His kingdom, soaking up everything in its path as we work together as a cohesive force to accomplish His perfect will on earth.

This same unity is also compared to dew that begins to form at the top of Mt. Hermon. This dew turned into a life-giving source of water for the fertile plains below. The small trickle of moisture which formed at the top would eventually grow into a significantly larger amount of water, sufficient to meet increasing needs along the way.

Both are beautiful analogies and combine to reveal God's ultimate plan for the church. When staff members firmly support the God-given vision of the lead pastor and as unity prevails in the church, the anointing will flow, the Water of Life, Jesus Christ, will cause everything to flourish. A greater number of people will inherit eternal life!

Tony Morgan once wrote candidly about the many times he left staff meetings in disagreement over a decision that had been made. He was greatly concerned about the impact it would have upon his team. Tony goes on to say:

> God is never glorified when division takes place in the local church as the result of a staff member's divisiveness.

"...as the number two guy, it is my responsibility to execute what has been decided, whether I like it or not. In these situations, I have a decision to make. Will I embrace it and make the decision my own, or will I pass the buck and blame the pastor in order to save face and/or avoid confrontation?"[3]

Throughout his extensive ministry experience, Tony learned the importance of supporting the pastor's vision, even when it differs from his own vision. He goes on to say:

"A true leader with a heart for unity will take a bullet for his pastor or supervisor. As a staff member, part of my job is to bear the ministry burdens and protect my pastor from the stress and conflict of unpopular decisions. A great number two staff owns the unpopular decisions and establishes himself as the leader in this situation"[4]

If we think about it, that is exactly the opposite response than what our initial human nature would dictate. How easy it would be for each of us to say, "This is exactly what I knew would happen – Pastor made that decision on his own, and it's going to bite him. There is no way I will take any responsibility for that. He's on his own!" It is incumbent upon all staff members to recognize their God-called role is to understand and support the vision of the primary leader. If a staff member sincerely cannot do that, they literally are in the wrong place and it is time to find an assignment elsewhere. To remain in that organization and be unable to honestly support the leader's vision would be detrimental and would undermine the spirit of unity which God desires to establish in that organization. As Brad Waggoner aptly says:

"As a second-chair leader, you have to genuinely care that

you are helping the first chair succeed."[5]

In closing, Proverbs 27:18 (NLT) offers a fitting word on this topic: *As workers who tend a fig tree are allowed to eat the fruit, so workers who protect their employer's interests will be rewarded.* When you support your leader's vision, you will be able to enjoy the success he or she experiences. You will be rewarded – if not directly by your leader, then certainly by God.

- **Reflect:** Have you been fully supportive of your leader's vision?

- **Receive:** Amos 3:3: *Can two people walk together without agreeing on the direction?* (NLT)

- **Respond:** Make a decision to be supportive of your leader's vision. Subsequently lay your vision down, so that his/her vision might be accomplished.

MY REFLECTIONS

CHAPTER 6

WILL YOU SURRENDER YOUR IDENTITY?

Jonathan and David made a covenant, because he loved him as his own soul.
And Jonathan took off the robe that was on him and gave it to David,
with his armor, even to his sword and his bow and his belt.
(1 Samuel 18:3-4)

THE word "surrender" means: *to stop resisting and to submit to another's authority; to give up.* It's a common challenge among staff members feeling they have no real identity in the church. There can be a nagging feeling that they have been swallowed up by the organization. They might feel pigeonholed to a tiny area of ministry, with all their ideas and potential contributions packed up in a box and tossed to the back storage area (next to the Christmas ornaments).

It is imperative for every staff member to recognize God did not call them to that local church with the primary goal of establishing and elevating their own identity. Rather, God called them to a specific place for a specific time to serve the greater good of that local body of believers. Here, they accomplish the plans God already had in mind. Doing so does not in any shape or form diminish the incredible talents and abilities of each man and woman of God on the staff. God has every intent of using your talents to the fullest. God has no intent of wasting the talents He gave you! He gifted you for a purpose, and we should celebrate those purposes. Nonetheless, we must recognize there are times and seasons in which God will require us to surrender our own identity for His greater glory.

Are you willing to do that?

Our society is diametrically opposed to this philosophy. The prevailing culture goes out of its way to embrace the concept of self-

> By giving his armor to David, Jonathan demonstrated a willingness to be vulnerable for David's sake. Jonathan's fear was not for his life, but for the life of David.

promotion, irrespective of the impact it has upon the greater good. The message is that our real identity is only found by taking all that we can for ourselves. Such a sentiment is incredibly short-sighted. On the contrary, as someone once said,

"There is no limit to the good a person can do if he doesn't care who gets the credit."[1]

As servants of Most High God, we each must ask ourselves, what is more important to us – getting credit in the here and now, or helping God build His kingdom for eternal glory?

If, as a secondary leader, it feels like you are sometimes asked to set aside your own agenda, you certainly are not alone. In fact, we find an incredible, almost unfathomable example of this in the account of David and Jonathan. The background of 1 Samuel chapter 18 is that Jonathan was the rightful heir to the throne of his father, King Saul. Nevertheless, Jonathan recognized and accepted the will of God for David's life, that he was the one whom God had chosen to succeed Saul.

By giving his robe to David, Jonathan, in effect surrendered his most precious identity to him. The robe symbolized his position as the son of King Saul. Perhaps no one would have confused David with Jonathan in terms of physical appearance, but when they saw the robe, it would be crystal clear that David was the rightful heir to the throne.

By giving his armor to David, Jonathan demonstrated a willingness to be vulnerable for David's sake. Jonathan's fear was not for his life, but for the life of David. Jonathan wanted to make sure David was protected at all times, even if it meant jeopardizing his own safety.

The lesson here is as amazing as it is unmistakable. Here we have a legitimate crown prince and legal, biological heir to the throne. There were no legal disputes concerning who should be the next king; no group of concerned citizens petitioned the king or high court to argue that someone else should have a chance. The line of succession was very clear. Because Jonathan saw God's mighty hand upon David and had such a great love for him, he was willing to abdicate his rightful position for God's greater glory. "Here, my wonderful friend David," you can almost hear him say. "Here is my robe, my royal robe. Take it, wear it, serve with distinction and integrity, and may the God of glory bless you richly as you serve Him as king in my place."

Coming from such a pure and honest motive, I don't know if we could find such an equivalent example in the world today; but that is precisely what Jonathan did. He was willing to sacrifice his own ideas, goals, plans, and even his identity as future king so that God's greater plans could be put into action. Observe there was no shame in Jonathan's actions. Indeed, I believe the eternal honor placed upon Jonathan in heaven far eclipses any temporal benefits he would have enjoyed while on earth.

For staff members, no one in the church or organization is likely be confused as to who you are or as to your role. Nevertheless, it is possible that very subtly and very gradually, you may lose sight of what is most important. The remedy is a genuine willingness to surrender your identity for the benefit of your primary leader.

Mike Bonem addresses this reality when he writes:

> Do not underestimate the power of unity, and do not underestimate God's ability to elevate you to whatever position He desires. Let that elevation be God's doing, rather than your own. When God elevates you, no one will be able to effectively derail you.

"Even though you're not the 'lead leader' and may do much of your work behind the scenes, you still have significant influence on the organization's success. If your church or ministry or non-profit is thriving, that's a strong indicator of your effectiveness. If it's not, you have a duty to determine why and to work on solutions."[2]

In the local church setting, even if people tell you that you should be the lead pastor, you preach better than he does, or they love you more than him, be willing to surrender your identity. Their confusion will be less likely to persist if you openly surrender your identity and support the greater vision of your leader.

This means you should always be willing to deflect the glory and the praise. For example, if someone expresses their appreciation for a message you preach, be sure to let them know that the only reason you could even bring the message is because the lead pastor affords you the privilege of being on the team. You should even take the next step and ask they let the lead pastor know their appreciation for your ministry gift. This in no way minimizes your contribution, but serves as a powerful means of building unity within the church by making it clear that it's not about you.

> Even if people tell you that you should be the lead pastor, you preach better than he does, or they even love you more than him, be willing to surrender your identity. Their confusion will be less likely to persist if you openly surrender your identity and support the greater vision of your leader.

Do not underestimate the power of unity, and do not underestimate God's ability to elevate you to whatever position He desires. Let that elevation be God's doing, rather than your own. When God elevates you, no one will be able to effectively derail you. Just like Jonathan saw a future king in his friend David, others will see God's hand on your life. There will be no real question that God has openly rewarded you for your incredible faithfulness. That is the place to be.

The world tends to get it backwards. Even the original disciples needed a lesson on the dangers of self-promotion. Matthew 20:27-28 records the Lord's response when the mother of James and John asked Him to allow her sons to sit right beside Him in special places of honor in His Kingdom. Now be honest, would you be embarrassed for someone in your family to show up at your workplace and ask your boss to give you a much nicer office? I think most people would be completely mortified, but that's exactly what happened! Knowing that the other ten disciples had become furious, Jesus replied, *Whoever desires to become great among you, let him be your servant. And whoever desires to be first among you, let him be your slave just as the Son of Man did not come to be served but to serve and to give His life a ransom for many.*

Philippians 2:5-6 says: *Your attitude should be the same that Christ Jesus had. Though He was God, He did not demand and cling to His rights as God. He made Himself nothing; He took the humble position of a slave and appeared in human form.* (NLT)

In keeping with this thought, Dick Hardy writes:

"Wise or foolish. Smart or not so smart. It's your choice. Think about it. If you could have all the wisdom and all the smarts in the world, wouldn't it be of high value to bring that to bear in lifting your senior pastor? If you do so, can you imagine what the long-range implication of the ministry could be? Think of how your individual ministry would advance."[3]

When everything within you screams out for recognition, be willing to remain in the shadows of obscurity. That is the essence of losing your identity. After all, Jesus was willing to do this, so we should do nothing less. As Psalm 75:6 reminds us: *...promotion and power come from nowhere on earth, but only from God.* (TLB)

Here is another reminder from Proverbs 25:6-7: *Don't work yourself into the spotlight; don't push your way into the place of prominence. It's better to be promoted to a place of honor than face humiliation by being demoted.* (MSG).

Two of the men who wrote an endorsement for this book are Dr. Sam Chand and Dr. Benson Karanja. I developed a deep appreciation for their leadership while attending Beulah Heights University in Atlanta. While they have different countries of origin – Dr. Chand is from India, Dr. Karanja is from Kenya – they have a similar path in some ways. Both men began attending the university in pursuit of an undergraduate degree. Both men served as janitor during their studies. Both men eventually became President of that same university. Both men were willing to surrender their identity, and both men have been tremendously rewarded by God.

When God elevates you, no one else can take your place. Think about that and be the best you can be right now.

- **Reflect:** Is your identity more important to you than it should be?

- **Receive:** John 1:19-20: *This is the testimony of John, when the Jews sent priests and Levites from Jerusalem to ask him, 'Who are you?' He confessed and did not deny, but confessed, 'I am not the Christ.'*

- **Respond:** Ask God to set you free from worrying about what others think of you. Focus solely on what He knows of you.

MY REFLECTIONS

CHAPTER 7

DO YOU UNDERSTAND WHAT YOUR LEADER IS DOING?

Jesus got up from the table, took off His robe, wrapped a towel
around His waist, and poured water into a basin. Then He began to wash
the disciples' feet and to wipe them with the towel He had around Him.
When He came to Simon Peter, Peter said to Him, "Lord, why are you
going to wash my feet?"
(John 13:4-6)

IN what must have been one of the most powerful and intimate moments during His earthly ministry, Jesus began to wash the feet of His disciples. As He did this, there was a great deal of confusion for some of those who were closest to Him. In particular, Peter failed to recognize what Jesus was really doing as He knelt to wash his feet. He missed the point so much that, after Jesus explained it to him, Peter would ask Him to wash his entire body instead of just his feet!

Confusion is not a gift from God; it is a tool of the devil. Whenever the staff is sufficiently confused about something, the collective strength of the team is reduced. This is perhaps never truer than when staff members fundamentally fail to understand what their leading seeks to accomplish. Despite his best efforts to communicate the mission, vision, and purpose of the church or organization, there are still times when some the staff members simply do not understand what their leader is doing.

We see this further exemplified as Jesus finished washing the feet of His disciples. In verse 21, He tells them, *One of you will betray Me.* Most of the disciples were horrified at such a thought, and immediately sought to identify the traitor in their midst. Jesus, certainly understanding their natural curiosity, revealed the answer by saying that the guilty party would be *the one to whom I give this crust of bread after I've dipped it* (verse 26). He then dipped the bread and handed it to Judas Iscariot.

You would think that at this point there would be no question in anyone's mind as to who will betray Jesus. He just made it crystal clear! He all but spray-painted "GUILTY" all over Judas' garment! Somehow, and to our perpetual amazement, the disciples remained utterly clueless. Later in the discussion, Jesus gave Judas some instructions, but observe, *No one around the supper table knew why He said this to him. Some thought that since Judas was their treasurer, Jesus was telling him to buy what they needed for the Feast, or that he should give something to the poor* (verses 28,29).

What? After Jesus outed Judas as His betrayer, they still didn't understand? Jesus just clearly told them that the one who would betray Him would be the person to whom he gave the bread, and without delay they all saw Him hand it to Judas! How much plainer could it possibly have been to them? Yet some of the disciples thought perhaps Jesus was trying to tell Judas to buy something from the store or to make a donation to help the poor.

You have got to be kidding me! How could they have missed what Jesus was saying? How could they have not clearly understood precisely what Jesus was doing? The annals of history are cluttered with the stories of individuals, families, and even churches failing to understand each other. How often have you been amazed that someone else thoroughly failed to understand "what you so clearly told them?" More importantly, what can we do to minimize the chance of this miscommunication?

> Whenever the staff is sufficiently confused about something, the collective strength of the team is reduced.

During my pastoral tenure, I remember sensing we should change the name of our church. The idea was something I considered for a long time and even kicked it around with Missy to get her thoughts. Over the course of many months, I believed I should discuss it with the pastoral and administrative staff. After talking and praying about it, we were in agreement that changing the name of the church was more than a good idea; it was a God idea. I then presented the idea to the board so that we, as the elected leaders, could fully vet the idea before proceeding any further. During our conversations, the board agreed, and the process was put into motion.

In accordance with our church governance, a proposed bylaw amendment was created and approved by the board. Since the name of the corporation was going to be changed, the official voting members must be given a chance to vote. The proposed bylaw amendment had to be read on the two Sundays prior to the business meeting and a copy had to be mailed to each voting member. All these steps are in accordance with our bylaws, ensuring that the matter is known to all and considered with full disclosure.

I remember quite vividly what took place after I read the proposed bylaw amendment and it received a second so that discussion could take place. As Chairman, it was my responsibility to address any questions which arose and to allow open dialogue to take place. There seemed to be a general sense of approval! Then, to my dismay...someone spoke in opposition to the name change. Not wanting to appear as if I was driving this decision, I did not respond to their concerns, and we moved to a vote. By majority vote, the decision to change the church name failed.

> For secondary leaders, the best way to know your primary leader comes through spending quality time with him. This way, you begin to understand his heart.

I was shocked. I was stunned. I had been convinced, along with the staff and the board, that this was the direction we should take as a church. What happened? What did I miss?

At our next staff meeting and board meeting, I made an open confession that the fault must lay at my feet. I had failed. My failure was neither intentional nor was it sinful. I had followed our bylaws to the letter. The technical requirements had been met. So, why did the name change fail? It failed because I had failed to clearly explain to the congregation the "why behind the what." Let me explain.

The whole church family had not been in the staff and board meetings. They weren't privy to the conversations which had taken place over the past several months. They had not heard all the answers to the questions which arose during those meetings. They had not been present when we discussed the pros and cons of changing the church name. They were given a chance to vote, and they did...but not how we expected.

The leadership agreed with a plan I proposed, which was to call for an informational meeting to present the idea again. The church family would be given a chance to ask more questions and receive clear answers. No votes would be taken, nor decisions made. We would just talk. It was refreshing and it was valuable. After a few months, we scheduled a business meeting and presented the name change once again. Having more time to understand the "why behind the what," the congregation voted to approve the new name. They understood, and they wholeheartedly agreed.

For secondary leaders, the best way to know your primary leader comes through spending quality time with him. This way, you begin to understand his heart. For example, be intentional about sharing a meal together, playing golf (or some other sport or mutually enjoyable activity), working on a special project together, and so on. Most importantly, have fun and laugh together! It will be during these times that you will gain a greater depth of insight into what your leader is passionate about, what they enjoy and what they would like to see happen within the organization. While that is true, here is a great reminder from Proverbs 25:8 when things aren't clear: *Don't jump to conclusions - there may be a perfectly good explanation for what you just saw.* (MSG)

If ever a primary leader would welcome a question, it is in the area of what he wants to see God accomplish within the church. "Maybe I should know this already, but what do you see happening in the next year? What are the top things you want God to do? How should we be preparing for these things?" Those types of questions give the leader a perfect opening to talk very plainly about what God has placed on his heart to accomplish, and a serious emphasis on those types of questions may very well assist you in growing within the organization.

- **Reflect:** How well do you understand what your leader is doing and where he or she wants to take your organization?

- **Receive:** Mark 2:7: *Why does this Man speak blasphemies like this? Who can forgive sins but God alone?*

- **Respond:** Make a decision to walk so closely with your leader that there will be no way you won't know what he or she is doing.

MY REFLECTIONS

CHAPTER 8

WILL YOU GO THE EXTRA MILE?

When you have done all those things which you are commanded, say,
We are unprofitable servants. We have done what was our duty to do.
(Luke 17:10)

AS staff members, there will be many, many, many times you are called upon to serve and to assist in areas that do not necessarily match your primary gifting, calling, or passion. I will give you a brief moment to get over your shock at that new revelation. What a blinding flash of the obvious! In ministry, this certainly happens all the time. It would not surprise me at all if it hasn't happened to you since breakfast this morning. The question for today is: are we willing to go the extra mile in service to our leader? It's a great question, and a very important one.

When hiring staff members for the past nineteen years, as I have reviewed their job description with them, I have stressed this reality by saying: "In addition to the duties outlined in the formal job description, on the back of the last page in invisible ink it reads, 'And anything else that I'm asked to do.'" There is a very good reason I like to bring that up with new additions to the staff. We always operate best as a team, and like a sports team we tend to have fairly well-defined roles within the church staff.

If this were a football team, we would not want two quarterbacks on the field at the same time, each calling different plays and trying to use different tactics against a powerful and well-organized opponent. We certainly want to show up each day and do the job we were called to do with excellence, fulfilling our part within the kingdom of God. Nevertheless, sometimes we will find ourselves serving in areas that are not our primary focus. The organization will be presented with countless ministry opportunities where there is no single, well-defined job description that covers them. When that occurs, your cooperation is both anticipated and appreciated. So, once again, the question of the day is:

are we willing to do that?

Jesus tells His disciples in Matthew 5:31: *If anyone compels you to go one mile, go with him two.* Jesus was telling them how to respond when a Roman soldier ordered them to do something. In other words, He expects this, even when the person you are serving may be perceived as an enemy!

Jesus completely upended the world's system. The foundation for this characteristic is summed up in one word - servanthood. True servants are always willing to go the extra mile because they fundamentally understand their role and the concept of serving. Hirelings, on the other hand, only do what they are paid to do. They sometimes fail miserably in grasping the concept of serving because they struggle with the perspective of, "I wasn't hired to do that!" or "That's not in my job description!" or "That's the youth pastor's job!"

As an associate pastor, one of my greatest joys came from knowing that everything I did was something that the lead pastor didn't have to do. Regardless of whether or not it was necessarily one of my assigned duties, I was thrilled to know he didn't have to focus his time and energy toward doing it.

Baseball players are not awarded the Golden Glove for simply showing up for the game; they are only recognized for going the extra mile. Singers are not given a Dove Award for simply recording a song; they are only recognized for going the extra mile. Actors do not receive an Academy Award for half-heartedly repeating a few lines on the set. In each of these cases, individuals receive enormous recognition only after going the extra mile. Not once, not twice, not when it is convenient or self-serving, but as a way of life. One trait which sets them apart is a consistent willingness to rise to the occasion, always eager to be the first person who arrives and the last to leave at the end of a long day.

> True servants are always willing to go the extra mile because they fundamentally understand their role and the concept of serving.

Do you truly want to rise above the ordinary? Are you willing to go the extra mile? Then make it a point to ask if there is anything else you can help the leader to do. Most staff members will perform their basic job requirements and they certainly may keep their jobs for a long time to come. The ones who receive the greatest rewards are those who are consistently willing to go the extra mile.

We live in an age where "participation trophies" are a thing.

Everyone being rewarded equally is not a principle we will find in scripture. If you look at it from a mathematical perspective, the three men in the parable of the talents each received a different percentage for their investment (or lack thereof). God can and will reward you immeasurably as you demonstrate a willingness to go above and beyond for the kingdom.

Merely fulfilling the most basic of your carefully assigned duties does not make you a hero, but from an eternal standpoint, going the extra mile does! Going the extra mile does not just mean when the leader is watching, either. Secondary leaders need to be counted on to do whatever needs to be done to ensure the smooth operation of the organization, regardless of whether anyone else appears to be watching at a given moment. As Brad Waggoner states,

> "We are called to availability, not specifically a certain label in a certain position."[1]

This is so true.

1 Samuel 18:5 says: *Whatever Saul gave David to do, he did it - and did it well. So well that Saul put him in charge of his military operations. Everybody, both the people in general and Saul's servants, approved of and admired David's leadership.* (MSG) Because David faithfully served Saul, he was elevated within the kingdom and other people trusted his capable leadership. Consider how wonderful it is and what a lasting tribute it is that for so many centuries believers have read about David's job well done. I would like for that to be said about me, and I believe you would, as well.

Genesis 39:2-6a further confirms the importance of going the extra mile: *The Lord was with Joseph, and he was a successful man; and he was in the house of his master the Egyptian. And his master saw that the Lord was with him and that the Lord made all he did to prosper* in his hand. *So, Joseph found favor in his sight, and served him. Then he made him overseer of his house, and all that he had he put under his authority. So it was, from the time that he had made him overseer of his house* and all that he had, *that the Lord blessed the Egyptian's house for Joseph's sake; and the blessing of the Lord was on* all that he had *in the house and in the field. Thus he left* all that he had *in Joseph's hand, and he did not know what he had except for the bread which he ate.* (emphasis added). As Joseph faithfully served Potiphar, God blessed everything that he did. Potiphar promoted him while providing him with greater and greater responsibilities.

Another beautiful example of this principle can be seen through the actions of three of David's mighty men in 1 Chronicles chapter 11. The background of this story is that David is hiding from King Saul who wrongly sought to take his life. While on the run, a group of men promptly came to David's aid, because they believed him to be wholly innocent of the charge of treason. They also believed he was God's clear choice to be their next king.

One day, while hiding in the cave of Adullam, the Bible records: *David said with longing, 'Oh, that someone would give me a drink of water from the well of Bethlehem, which is by the gate!' So the three broke through the camp of the Philistines, drew water from the well of Bethlehem that was by the gate, and took it and brought it to David. Nevertheless, David would not drink it, but poured it out to the Lord. And he said, 'Far be it from me, O my God, that I should do this! Shall I drink the blood of these men who have put their lives in jeopardy? For at the risk of their lives they brought it.' Therefore he would not drink it.*

Will you go the extra mile for someone today?

Although he had a much larger number of mighty men who served and protected him, on this particular day, there were only three who were willing to go the extra mile for David. As it is today, it seems that doing so was the exception rather than the rule. What made those three men so different than the rest of David's mighty men was an extraordinary level of devotion and commitment to their primary leader. What can we learn from their example? If we truly wish to set ourselves apart, we may do so by going the extra mile.

Jesus also taught on the importance of going the extra mile through the parable of the talents in Matthew chapter 25. As you may recall, a wealthy man gave different sums of money to three different servants to keep while he went on a journey. Upon his return, the man called the three servants to give an account of what they had done with his money. Unfortunately, one man hid the money and only gave the man back the same amount of money that he had received. The man told him, *You wicked and lazy servant...you ought to have deposited my money with the bankers, and at my coming I would have received back my own with interest.*

On the contrary, the other two men invested wisely and gave the man back twice as much as they originally received. In both cases these servants were told, *Well done, good and faithful servant; you were faithful over a few things, I will make you ruler over many things.* It should be obvious to us that the way we handle someone else's possessions will have a significant impact upon our own future with the company where we are employed.

Ecclesiastes 9:10 states: *Work hard at whatever you do...* (TEV) The heartbreaking reality is that not every person heeds this admonition. In fact, there seem to be very few who take this to heart.

According to Calvin Miller, in *The Empowered Leader – 10 Keys to Servant Leadership:*

> "Less than one of four working people now say that they are working at full potential. Half of the current workforce say that they do not put any more effort into a job than they absolutely must do to keep the job. Three-fourths of the American workforce say they could be more effective and almost 60% agree that they do not work as hard as they used to work."[2]

Unfortunately, according to Eric Chester, Founder and CEO of RevivingWorkEthic.com, the future doesn't look much brighter:

> "America's emerging workforce - those in the sixteen-to-twenty-four age bracket - bring some amazing skill sets and personality traits into the labor pool. The challenge is that Millennials don't always want to work, and when they do, their terms don't always line up with those of their employers."[3]

When asked what tip he would give to help someone to become a more motivated worker, Chester replied:

> "Work like you're showing off...as if your every move is being video recorded...and that your parents, kids, friends and future employers are all tuned-in. If you perform your normal job as you would under these conditions for an entire day...it will be impossible for your employers not to notice you. Very soon, you will be the very best at your job, and once you are, you will be promoted, you will see a dramatic increase in your pay, and you will be sought out by other employers. When you are the best at your job, your future is unstoppable."[4]

Chick-fil-A has a corporate policy known as "Second Mile/Second

Nature." Chick-fil-A instills within their employees that it should be second nature to go the second mile for their customers. I also understand that Chick-fil-A has a sticker with "SMSN" printed on it, which they affix to food items that require "special attention" (e.g. – especially prepared) or that are being served because of "special circumstances" (e.g. – difficult customer). They do this to remind employees that going the second mile should be second nature to them, and not an inconvenience.

Missy and I have a dear friend who owns a wonderful restaurant, which we have frequented many times. The food is delicious and the service she personally provides is exceptional. Suffice it to say, we always leave full, satisfied, and encouraged each time we dine there! During one visit, this precious lady told us the restaurant business can be very demanding while also being extremely fulfilling at the same. The difficulties, she went on to say, are usually people-oriented, because some people are extremely hard to satisfy. Our friend then made a comment that we had not anticipated when she said, "I have to admit that Chick-fil-A is not my favorite restaurant as far as the food is concerned, but I will tell you this. After I've had a really hard day in my restaurant, I'll go through the drive-thru at Chick-fil-A and order a sweet tea just so I can hear somebody tell me, 'It's my pleasure to serve you!' because that really picks me up!"

Wow. Will you go the extra mile for someone today?

- **Reflect:** When was the last time you went the extra mile, without even being asked?

- **Receive:** Proverbs 12:24: *Work hard and become a leader; be lazy and become a slave.* (NLT)

- **Respond:** Look for ways you can go above and beyond your job description to serve your leader more effectively.

MY REFLECTIONS

CHAPTER 9

WILL YOU BE AN ENCOURAGER?

...encourage the fainthearted...
(1 Thessalonians 5:14, NRSV)

THE word "encourage" means "to inspire with courage, spirit or confidence." In practical terms, you are an encourager when you give support, hope or courage to your primary leader – especially in times of great adversity or difficulty. Everyone who has been in leadership for fifteen minutes knows that serving other people can sometimes be very challenging and even downright discouraging. Difficult counseling sessions, tough meetings, leadership deficiencies, limited finances, and countless other things can all take their toll on ministers. It is an ironic occupational hazard that the very ministers who devote their lives to encouraging others often find themselves in a place of great personal discouragement.

Let's look at a familiar example from scripture. Exodus 17:11-13 says: *And so it was, when Moses held up his hand that Israel prevailed and when he let down his hand, [his enemy] Amalek prevailed. But Moses' hands became heavy, so they took a stone and put it under him and he sat on it. And Aaron and Hur supported his hands, one on one side and the other on the other side, and his hands were steady until the going down of the sun. So Joshua defeated Amalek and his people with the edge of the sword.*

This is one of the clearest instances of how tangible, meaningful encouragement was given by two secondary leaders (Aaron and Hur) to their primary leader (Moses). God called Moses to a particular task, but he was humanly incapable of fulfilling that assignment entirely on his own. God does that a lot, doesn't He? He gives someone a task that is far too great for a single individual. That is where Aaron and Hur come into the picture. Moses saw Israel winning when his hands were up, and saw Israel losing when his hands were down. For whatever reason, he clearly

61

recognized their victory was directly connected to his ability to keep his hands raised.

You may be familiar with how Aaron and Hur helped Moses on this fateful day, but have you ever considered what would have happened if Aaron and Hur had responded differently? What if Aaron tried to force Moses to the side, so he could take over and make a greater name for himself? Do you think God would have been honored? Do you think Israel would have won the battle that day? Thankfully, Aaron and Hur were not confused about God's assignment for them: hold Moses' hands up.

Nowhere does Scripture record Aaron lamenting, "Good grief, where exactly in my job description does it say I have to hold up someone's arm? I didn't sign up for this!" They did not struggle with or complain about the fact that their sole assignment that day was simply to support Moses as he fulfilled his God-given responsibilities. While Israel's victory is directly connected to Moses' obedience, the truth is that Israel's victory was also connected to the encouragement that Aaron and Hur were willing to extend to Moses.

Historians may view the victory that day as made possible through Moses' faithful leadership. But without the rock-solid support of his secondary leadership team, there would have been no victory. Israel would have suffered a crushing defeat at the hands of their enemies.

Keep that in mind as you help your leader fight whatever battles the day may bring. Quite often you will not be fully aware of all the battles your leader faces, even if you think you have a pretty good idea. Your encouragement and support mean all the more to your leader because you bring your resources to each situation - more than the leader can bring on their own. It is not good for leaders to lead alone – they need you right alongside them bringing your unique skills, talents, strength, and ideas to the task at hand. It sometimes is, indeed, the difference between victory and defeat.

> It is not good for leaders to lead alone – they need you right alongside them bringing your unique skills, talents, strength, and ideas to the task at hand. It sometimes is, indeed, the difference between victory and defeat.

A difficult dynamic faced by primary leaders is that they feel they have no one to turn to for encouragement. It is often intimidating and embarrassing for a leader to admit to a staff member that they feel discouraged. It is virtually impossible for a leader to confide in a member of the organization that they are discouraged. Think about it – if you were the lead pastor, so full of the Holy Spirit and so fresh off last week's powerful sermon on victorious living for Christ, how keen would you be to admit to anyone in the congregation that you are barely hanging on for dear life? Would you not feel like a hypocrite in doing so, rather than as a human being who has recently been pounded by life's storms?

In 1 Samuel 30, David and his men return from battle to Ziklag to find their enemy burned their homes, stole their valuables, and even took their precious families captive. As a result of their great discouragement and abject pain, David's men talked about stoning him to death. Thankfully, 1 Samuel 30:6 records, *But David encouraged himself in the Lord.* To his credit, David was able to encourage himself in the Lord...but it sure would have been nice to have someone else to walk with him on that terrible day. Where were his encouragers?

Standing beside a leader to provide real encouragement is one of the most beneficial things a staff member can do. Maybe things seem to be going pretty well at the moment. Maybe the leader is riding high on a series of great personal victories. Do not limit your encouragement to the times of great visible difficulty within the organization. Remain cognizant of the strong likelihood of multiple battles being waged beneath the surface. Being an encourager is most definitely a 24/7/365 assignment and privilege for staff members. It assuredly is a solemn responsibility that none of us should take lightly.

In Acts chapter 4, the New Testament church had all things in common because everyone shared all they had with anyone in need. Verses 36-37 tell us: *Joseph, who was also surnamed Barnabas by the apostles (which is translated Son of Encouragement) a Levite of the country of Cyprus, having land, sold it and brought the money and laid it at the apostle's feet.* Did you catch that? His birth name was Joseph, but he had such a habit of encouragement that the apostles gave him a new name that means "Son of Encouragement." This wasn't a one-time or occasional post on social media where Barnabas tried to lift up someone else. He made a lifestyle of encouraging others. He put his money where his mouth was! He literally sold some land and gave the proceeds to the apostles.

Soon after Paul's dramatic conversion on the road to Damascus, it

> Standing beside a leader to provide real encouragement is one of the most beneficial things a staff member can do.

was Barnabas who stood up and courageously defended Paul to put to rest the church's suspicions that Paul's conversion was actually a trap. In ways great and small, this servant leader left a huge and lasting impact upon other leaders because he fundamentally understood the art of encouragement.

A simple way of encouraging the lead pastor can be to let him know you enjoyed his sermon. He may have spent many hours preparing the message and there may have been very little visible response from the people. A kind remark and a little encouragement may be just what he needs before returning to the pulpit or preparing for his next counseling session. Proverbs 12:25 reminds us: *Worry weighs a person down; an encouraging word cheers a person up.* (NLT) The rank-and-file members of the congregation are not the only ones who need the full benefit of God's Word when it comes to encouragement or any other topic. The primary leader needs it every bit as much!

Before we conclude this chapter, let me share with you something Dr. Todd Smith wrote regarding the need to pray for your pastor:

> "The pressure on pastors and their families is enormous and unprecedented. Due to many factors, pastors face an onslaught of discouragement, self-doubt, and unbridled frustration. In addition, many have to confront dark and debilitating depression. These attacks and others like them lead to burnout, and thus, many good men and women leave the ministry altogether. One thing is clear: the devil has a ferocious appetite for pastors, their families and church leaders. Since pastors are on the front lines of the battle for the souls of men, they are prime targets for the devil. The enemy knows that when a leader falls or quits, it demoralizes their followers and hinders the cause of Christ in their area. Please take time each day to pray in the spirit for your pastors and their families. Your prayers could be the very thing that keeps them moving forward, led out of temptation or even from quitting. Satan knows if he can devastate the leadership of a church or ministry, then the likelihood of a sustainable move of God taking place through their work is unlikely."[1]

This week, resolve to find an appropriate way to provide real encouragement to your leader. Never underestimate the impact your words will have.

Those are sobering words. Will you be an avid encourager to your primary leader?

You may or may not view yourself as much of a writer, but would you like to make a lasting impact upon your leader? Write him a letter of encouragement. It can be a single page or just a few pages, but make the time to do this and share just how much his leadership has meant to you. Include something specific the leader has said or done that has really lifted you up or blessed your family. Express your appreciation for what he has done for others, perhaps in situations you have witnessed where you know someone else was helped because of their care and concern. Simple text messages and posts on social media are great, but in this case, take the time to write a letter and quietly place it on his desk. Trust me when I say that such a letter will mean a thousand times more than you liking his post about an upcoming message. When received out of the blue and outside the context of a birthday or annual Pastor's Appreciation Sunday, this type of communication delivers a strong and lasting source of encouragement the leader can pull out on occasion when the going is especially tough.

Don't delay. This week, resolve to find an appropriate way to provide real encouragement to your leader. Never underestimate the impact your words will have.

- **Reflect:** How much better would your primary leader be able to lead if you were to regularly encourage him or her?

- **Receive:** Proverbs 25:11: *The right word at the right time is like precious gold set in silver.* (CEV)

- **Respond:** Look for ways where you can go above and beyond your job description to more effectively serve your leader.

MY REFLECTIONS

CHAPTER 10

ARE YOU CONTENT WITH YOUR CALLING?

*The Lord said to Samuel, "You have mourned long enough for Saul.
I have rejected him as king of Israel. Now fill your horn with olive oil
and go to Bethlehem. Find a man named Jesse who lives there,
for I have selected one of his sons to be my new king."*
(1 Samuel 16:1)

BEING content with your calling means you are happy or satisfied with what God has assigned for you to do in His kingdom. Although you may aspire to do other things as the Lord sovereignly open those doors in His timing, you remain focused on performing (to the best of your abilities) your current assignment. Being content with your calling also means you do not allow yourself to be distracted by or envious of other leaders who may have different giftings or a larger platform.

1 Samuel chapter 16 records how God rejected King Saul and placed the anointing on David to become Israel's next king. Although he was anointed, the reality is that David did not immediately pack up his bags and travel with great fanfare to the throne room. In fact, after being anointed David went right back into the fields to watch his father's sheep instead of occupying the king's palace. What exactly was his progression from the fields to the palace?

David started out as a lowly shepherd boy who later was promoted to delivery boy through a simple assignment to take food to his brothers where they waited across from the valley where the Philistines had assembled for war. From his stint as a delivery boy, he was then promoted to giant killer. From giant killer, he eventually became the king. We see the journey from the pasture to the palace was one that included multiple promotions. One of those promotions may have taken place very quickly, but overall, the journey was exceedingly difficult and took place over the course of many years.

Let's be honest: that isn't quite the way we would like things to happen, is it? If we could map out our ideal path to success, the journey almost invariably would be much easier, happen much more quickly, and contain far fewer painful setbacks. Right?

In mapping out his personal strategy for a triumphant arrival in the Promised Land, Moses would not have said to himself, "It would be so great if I could lead millions of grumbling, complaining Israelites through the desert for forty years." Joseph would not have concocted a plan

> Some people have unique skills to be primary leaders while some people have equally unique skills to be secondary leaders.

to be falsely accused of raping his boss's wife and then spend years in a filthy jail. Even Jesus, praying as if His life depended on it the night before His arrest, asked the Father if it was possible for that particular cup (that particular trial) to be taken away. In each of these cases, we find a willingness to remain faithful to the task at hand, even when the stakes are high and the pain levels are turned up to the max.

That isn't quite the way we would like things to play out. While David remained exceptionally faithful to God, Absalom (one of David's own sons) was unwilling to learn the valuable lesson from his father's life. He had a front-row seat to the life of one of the greatest men who ever lived. He should have been positioned to carry on David's strong legacy of personal integrity and closeness to God. Instead, he would tragically promote himself without waiting on God's process to be completed.

Second Samuel 15:1-6 records this story by saying: *After this, Absalom bought a chariot and horses, and he hired fifty bodyguards to run ahead of him. He got up early every morning and went out to the gate of the city. When people brought a case to the king for judgment, Absalom would ask where in Israel they were from, and they would tell him their tribe. Then Absalom would say, "You've really got a strong case here! It's too bad the king doesn't have anyone to hear it. I wish I were the judge. Then everyone could bring their cases to me for judgment, and I would give them justice!" When people tried to bow before him, Absalom wouldn't let them. Instead, he took them by the hand and kissed them. Absalom did this with everyone who came to the king for judgment, and so he stole the hearts of all the people of Israel.* (NLT)

We see God Himself anointed and appointed David to serve as the next king of Israel. God chose David and divinely set in motion a series of events to pave the way for David to accomplish His perfect plans for that nation. In stark contrast, Absalom not only coveted his father's position, he also strategically sought to overthrow him and take the throne by force. Talk about selfish ambition!

Note again the contrast here, beginning with David's humility and patience as he waited for God's plans to unfold. He was perfectly willing to continue herding sheep until the time was right. In 2 Samuel 15 we read how Absalom bought a horse and chariot and hired fifty bodyguards to run ahead of him. We can see the shameless acts of self-promotion followed by the cunning way in which he manipulated those who were seeking justice. All this to overthrow his own father!

We are not talking about a minor slip-up over which Absalom subsequently repented. This was an ongoing pattern of willful subversion. Eventually, it led to a revolt in which thousands of people lost their lives, including Absalom himself. For whatever reason, Absalom was not content with his father as king and he was not content with his own calling. His covetousness cost him his life, along with the lives of those who stood with him. We are wise to take heed of these tragic lessons lest we in any small way be tempted to follow in his footsteps.

Another important example of remaining content with your calling appears in Exodus chapter 31. God is telling Moses exactly how the Tabernacle was to be built. God provides Moses two skilled secondary leaders to help with the work. More specifically, we read in Exodus 31:1-6 (emphasis added), *Then the Lord said to Moses, 'Look, I have specifically chosen Bezalel son of Uri, grandson of Hur, of the tribe of Judah. I have filled him with the Spirit of God, giving him great wisdom, ability, and expertise in all kinds of crafts. He is a master craftsman, expert in working with gold, silver, and bronze. He is skilled in engraving and mounting gemstones and in carving wood. He is a master at every craft! And I have personally appointed Oholiab son of Ahisamach, of the tribe of Dan, to be his assistant. Moreover, I have given special skill to all the gifted craftsmen so they can make all the things I have commanded you to make...'"* Interestingly enough, even though they created all of the items used in the Tabernacle, Bezalel and Oholiab would never use any of them because they were not Levitical priests.

Some people have unique skills to be primary leaders while some people have equally unique skills to be secondary leaders. The latter are the folks whose name will never appear on the company's letterhead, and they are OK with that. They do not have to be in the limelight because they know their place is in the shadows. In fact, many of those secondary leaders do not even aspire to be the primary leader, because they are comfortable in their own skin. They do not see the need to "move up" the corporate ladder; they are content with their position.

Is it inherently wrong for a staff member to desire to one day be the leader? Of course not. I want to be very careful not to put a damper on anything God may have placed on your heart to accomplish. It is true that we all have to start somewhere, and if God has placed on your heart a genuine desire to lead one day, then I will not only respect that, I will also stand with you in prayer that He will open the right doors at the right time. While there may be no harm in a staff member desiring to serve as a primary leader one day, understand there is an imminent danger in desiring such an office before God opens the door. If a staff member covets his or her leader's office, then that person is struggling with the "Absalom nature" lurking within. The result may seem justifiable, but the means to accomplish it are entirely wrong and contrary to God's will. As Byrd Baggett noted:

> While there may be no harm in a staff member desiring to serve as a primary leader one day, understand there is an imminent danger in desiring such an office before God opens the door. If a staff member covets his or her leader's office, then that person is struggling with the "Absalom nature" lurking within.

"What is buried within your heart will devour and destroy you from within."[1]

Eric Geiger addresses this truth in an article entitled *The Peter Principle and the Saul Syndrome*:

"Greater responsibility tends to expose cracks in one's character. The cracks were already there, but the added burden or the additional 'power' made them more visible. If people are promoted based on their skill alone, they are promoted into a place where a lack of integrity will be more damaging to others."[2]

The sad reality is that some people are not content with their calling. For them, promotion often leads to corruption. We must guard against this spirit of Absalom which has no place within God's kingdom.

While serving in various associate roles, people would ask me when I thought God would place me in a position of lead pastor. Each time, my response was the same: I was neither running to that nor was I running from that. Until it happened and God sovereignly opened the door, I was content with the assignment He had given to me. It is only human to want to hurry things up sometimes and get to the greener grass that surely must be on the other side. Be very careful what you wish for, because it is far better to wait in the wings a few more years while you develop greater spiritual maturity and organizational skills than to be handed the reins of an entire church before you truly are ready.

No one wants to end up "way over their heads," especially since everyone else can tell when someone is in such a plight. Indeed, many primary leaders have openly expressed how priceless their earlier struggles and pesky setbacks were to their ministry. They have based entire sermons around them to demonstrate God's great faithfulness and perfect planning. In the final analysis, those tough times were instrumental in shaping primary leaders in ways that would adequately prepare them for the challenges ahead. Even the seasons of apparent defeat had a crucial role to play. It has been said that sometimes God allows you to experience defeat to toughen you up for a greater battle and a greater victory.

Returning once more to the stark contrast between David and Absalom, which path will you choose? A hundred years from now, how do you want your legacy to read? Will it contain a timeless reminder that God in His graciousness elevated you over a period of many years to a position of honor within the kingdom? Or will it lament that you led a revolt within your organization to take for yourself what God had intended for another? Will it track your steady progress from position to position as God grooms you for something greater, or will it show how your lack of confidence in your primary leader led you to gather other disgruntled people to your cause?

Do not lose sight of the fact that God indeed has plans for a greater victory for you. I do not know what shape or form that might take, but I do know that Lamentations 3:22-23 is spot on: *The steadfast love of the Lord never ceases; His mercies never come to an end; they are new every morning; great is Your faithfulness.* Remain true to God, and He will remain true to you. He will establish you in all your ways according to His perfect plans. When all is said and done, you will not want anything other than His perfect plans for your life. It will indeed be worth the wait.

- **Reflect:** Are you truly content with the calling God has for your life?

- **Receive:** 2 Peter 1:10: *Therefore, brethren, be even more diligent to make your call and election sure, for if you do these things you will never stumble.*

- **Respond:** Begin to thank God for placing you right where He needs you to be so you can fulfill His mandate upon your life.

MY REFLECTIONS

CHAPTER 11

WILL YOU MINISTER TO YOUR LEADER?

Jehoshaphat said, "Is there no prophet of the Lord here that we may inquire of the Lord by him?" So one of the servants of the king of Israel answered and said, "Elisha the son of Shaphat is here who poured water on the hands of Elijah." And Jehoshaphat said, "The Word of the Lord is with him."
(2 Kings 3:11-12)

MINISTERING to people is the core job requirement of every church staff member. It is at the very heart of what we do. It would be absurd to think about how a church could operate effectively without the entire staff devoted to ministry in some shape or form. We did not sign up to be served, but to serve! I believe we each understand this basic truth, but somehow during the process it can be easy to lose sight of it. Sometimes we mistakenly view the lead pastor as the one who is supposed to do all the ministering. After all, he (or she) is "the minister." He may even have "minister" neatly included in his official title and printed on business cards. Obviously, "the minister" is supposed to do the ministering, right?

Right. But he needs to receive ministry, as well.

Take a quick moment and think of your favorite restaurant. Ask yourself, does the chef need to eat? After whipping up his latest New Orleans-inspired dish and placing it with a grand flourish on table nine, does he not get hungry and need nourishment to keep going? It is his job to feed others, but if he doesn't do some eating of his own, he will be of little use to anyone else. We could also consider our doctors and how many patients they see, in one day's work. We, of course, greatly appreciate the medical care they provide. We also understand that sometimes doctors get sick, too. They need medicine, surgery, post-operative care, rest, and plenty of liquids, just like the rest of us!

Ministers need ministry, too. God says what you provide to others will be provided to you, as we can see from Proverbs 11:25: *The generous will prosper; those who refresh others will themselves be refreshed.*

In an earlier chapter, I mentioned a friend who owns a restaurant. Recall that after a hard day's work, she would occasionally swing by another restaurant for the sole purpose of hearing someone else say, "It's my pleasure to serve you!" She said that really picks her up and boosts her spirits.

We can easily witness this truth in scripture, seeing how great leaders have received ministry from others. In 1 Chronicles 11:17-20, we find three of David's mighty men risked their lives to minister to him. They brought him water while a band of enemy Philistines was camped nearby. David's canteen had been dry for some time in the hot desert.

We see how the standing of a man named Joseph rose to the point where the apostles gave him a truly wonderful nickname. What did this man do to merit such a distinctive honor? Acts chapter 4 records the apostles called him Barnabas, which means "Son of Encouragement." The apostles themselves were leaders who dearly appreciated the constant encouragement of this brother in the faith. His ministry to them meant so much, they gave him a new name. Such an action was highly significant in that culture.

> Ministers absolutely need ministering. Your primary leader is no exception.

Even our Lord Jesus needed ministering. Matthew 4:11 records that after being tempted by the devil, angels came and ministered to Him. As He prayed on the Mount of Olives before His arrest, an angel came to strengthen Him (Luke 22:43). We can even point to Mary's example in John 12:3 where she poured expensive perfume on the feet of Jesus, wiping His feet dry with her hair. Speaking of feet, Jesus loved to demonstrate important truths by example, and He did so in John 13:1-17. The disciples would go on to be key leaders who would change the course of history by spreading the good news of God's kingdom. Jesus showed them by example, ministering to them as He washed their feet and taught them to do the same.

Through these examples, we clearly see the proof. Ministers absolutely need ministering. Your primary leader is no exception. Look again at 2 Kings 3:11-12: *Jehoshaphat said, 'Is there no prophet of the Lord here that we may inquire of the Lord by him?' So one of the servants of the king of Israel answered and said, 'Elisha the son of Shaphat is here* who poured water on the hands of Elijah.' *And Jehoshaphat said, 'The Word of the Lord is with him.'* (emphasis added)

Here we find Elisha was known by reputation for two basic things:

First, he was known as a prophet of God. Second, he was known as having ministered to Elijah. As a result, the people were convinced the Word of the Lord was with him.

This passage sheds light on an overlooked lesson: in ministering to your primary leader, other people's confidence in your leadership will increase. They will more easily recognize you are a man or woman of God and that God's Word is with you. As a result, both your standing and your potential of leading them will increase. Look how this must have impacted Jehoshaphat, the king of Judah. I do not know if prior to this passage the king knew anything about Elisha or if he had even heard the name. When he learned Elisha had ministered to Elijah, he immediately responded with certainty: *The Word of the Lord is with him* (v.12). When you minister to your primary leader, that same dynamic will come into play. Your standing with others will increase. We see from Jehoshaphat's example that this can and will leave a very strong impression on others.

> Take care to consider your motives when spending time with your primary leader. While ministering to him will elevate you in the eyes of others, such an elevation should not be the underlying motive.

Consider how Acts chapter 4 relates the account of Peter and John appearing before the Sanhedrin. This ruling class was greatly disturbed, as the apostles were teaching and proclaiming Jesus' resurrection from the dead. The Sanhedrin was made up of elders, eminent scholars, and rabbis —a powerful group of leaders with great religious and political power. By the Sanhedrin's own observations, Peter and John were merely "unschooled, ordinary men." (My contemporary interpretation of that phrase is Peter and John were "ignorant and inexperienced," but that's not very respectful, so please disregard!)

As we read the passage, we note members of the Sanhedrin were astonished at the enormous wisdom, clarity, and power exhibited by Peter and John as they stood before them. Observe closely: *...they took note that these men had been with Jesus.* (Acts 4:13) Their mere proximity to Jesus caused this powerful group of men to look at Peter and John with new eyes. There was something different about them they had not seen before. Such will be the natural outgrowth of your careful and consistent attention to minister to your primary leader.

While this is such a powerful concept on leadership, take care to consider your motives when spending time with your primary leader.

While ministering to him will elevate you in the eyes of others, such an elevation should not be the underlying motive. A church version of climbing the corporate ladder should not be the driving factor behind such ministry. We find elsewhere that the Pharisees prayed publicly, so as to receive the attention of men. In response, Jesus said that was all the reward they would ever receive. Let your heart and motive be to honor God by honoring your primary leader. God will take care of the rest.

Jesus tells us in Matthew 23:11-12: *The greatest among you must be a servant. But those who exalt themselves will be humbled, and those who humble themselves will be exalted.*

Pastor Eric Todd, The Transformation House (transformationhouse.org): "For those of you who don't know, being a new Pastor (or seasoned Pastor) can sometimes be a long and lonely journey! You spend a lot of one-on-one time with God. You have numerous church responsibilities where you are either leading or managing throughout the year. You have family responsibilities. You have life responsibilities of your own. And lastly, you are constantly shepherding and pouring out to your church in some capacity every week. Even though you love those lifegiving experiences with all your heart, you can still find yourself feeling all alone, on this road called ministry, because you're constantly serving others. When you feel like that, who ministers to you? Or a better question will be, when life is constantly happening and coming at you from every single direction, who ministers to the minister, so the minister can receive, what he or she freely gives to others?

"For me, that answer is simple, Pastor Shell Osbon of Life Church. He has been that servant, that shepherd and that minister for me in times of need – when I too needed support. I could tell you of when, out of the blue, he emailed and asked me to call him so he could welcome me and The Transformation House to the community. I could tell you of when he invited me to a Life Church revival service, how he called my wife and I upfront to tell our story and to bless us with a financial contribution to support our ministry (and it continued every month for two consecutive years). Or I could tell you how we have met up for coffee on several occasions just so he can see how I'm doing. And finally, I could just tell you how he calls and texts me regularly to see how I am doing, to see if I need anything, to keep abreast of what is happening in the community and to remind me that he is always available if I need anything. I could go on and on and on, telling you how he has ministered to me and how that has helped me as a person, husband, father and as a pastor. But none of that would mean anything if he wasn't available and didn't have a servant's heart. He has been available to minister to me because God knew I needed it. He truly symbolizes and embodies Mark 10:45 where Jesus said, 'For even the Son of Man came not to be served but to serve.'"

Pastors Larry and Jennifer Grawey, Kennesaw Family Life Church (kennesawfamilylifechurch.org): "We have been in full time ministry for more than 25 years and have had many seasons where our tank has begun to run dry. Several years ago, we served at a church that was very demanding as well as working full-time with foster families. God had moved us from Florida to Georgia to start a church, but mentally we were worn out. Through the grace of the Holy Spirit, we were led to take a year off and were ministered to by the staff of Life Church. Getting ready to step into a position as primary leaders, it was important that we take the time to be ministered to in order to prepare us to launch a new church. The leadership team at Life Church did just that. Pastor Shell and the entire Life Church family continue to be a source of encouragement and strength. Church planting is draining on many levels. You are not only the primary leaders. Many times, you are also the secondary leaders. This takes its toll on your ability to minister to the people God has called you to. Looking back, there have been several times that Life Church has opened their doors to us as primary leaders of another church and ministered to us.

"In 2017, there was a revival going on at Life Church. Knowing that ministers need being ministered to, Pastor invited us and many other primary leaders to come and be refreshed. We attended several of these services and were not only ministered to but prophesied over. God used that time to put a new spark into our ministry and to encourage us in a time where we were feeling worn out and defeated. The Life Church staff continues to be a source of encouragement and are always willing to minister to us. In turn, we can better minister to the people of our community because we are working from a full tank instead of an empty one."

Pastor Jerauld and Anna Rekow, River of Life (riveroflifemenomonie.com): Pastor Jerauld says, "I know we wouldn't be where we are right now if it wasn't for other leaders pouring into us. Pastor Shell and Missy Osbon and Life Church Smyrna have been instrumental in supporting us in our senior leadership journey. They believed in us and gave opportunities before senior leadership positions became available for us. Through encouraging words, financial blessings and practical ideas, they have shown us that they have been in our corner. Additionally, because of their examples, in our current role we have sought out other leaders to support and encourage. Those leaders have in turn been a support for us. It can be lonely at the top but we have been blessed to have amazing leaders who are a little further down the road who have been cheering for us during the race set before us."

Anna goes on to say, "You welcomed us like family from the moment we stepped inside the church. It was like coming home. It was a Holy Spirit connectedness that only He can secure in hearts that are in transition. You and a team from the church helped us move into our little apartment. You prayed over our family as we purchased our first home and stood together in that new home as we dedicated ourselves to Him. We knew God had placed us there in that community for His extraordinary purposes. You treated our son Silas (and really ALL the children) just like Jesus. You'd kneel down at their level and would spend time genuinely engaging them in conversation. Silas would always smile even if he didn't always have the words. You gave us an office to use for the missions organization we were serving at the time. We eventually began serving as your young adults leaders and were encouraged by your constant prayers and support in the process. You knew when we needed extra encouragement and would treat us to lunch to have more opportunity to mentor us. Your church hosted a doctor who would bring information to me that seemed to align with my concerning symptoms. It was just the right timing to start what I didn't know then was the realization of ovarian cancer. Healthcare and wellness within the church were priorities and that was just what I needed. You, Missy and the church prayed me through several tests and surgeries. Those hours in hospital waiting rooms with you both beside us during such an unknown time was a defining moment for me. You brought an assurance that only the presence of Jesus can settle in a concerned heart. You also hosted missionaries, special speakers and evangelists who fine-tuned and redirected my focus in life and in ministry. I learned that God truly had a good purpose in mind all along and I was being used by Him even in my suffering. I was healed in my body, soul and spirit many times at those altars. You rejoiced with us when we were blessed with the surprising miracle of our daughter. Only God knew the importance and timing of these defining moments: 8/2011 - removal of stage 1A granulosa cell ovarian tumor; 10/2011 - staging surgery and removal of left ovary/fallopian tube; 7/2012 - 9 months later - a miracle baby detected; 3/2013 - miracle baby arrived healthy and beautiful. You and Missy physically and prayerfully stood by our side at every twist and turn. The preaching and leadership opportunities given to Jerauld were all part of a bigger plan to launch us back into full time ministry. I always appreciated your transparency and how you'd say, "Hi, my name is Shell. I'm your friend and I'm a human just like you. We share the same struggles as you do." That was such a comfort to hear. You made the altar a place I wanted to be. No guilt... just surrender. No shame... just tenderness. No games... just conversation. No agenda... just uninterrupted face-in-the-carpet time with Jesus. The community partnerships/involvement were essential to the application of what we heard and experienced on Sundays. We learned that it truly takes a team to successfully accomplish special events/outreaches. The love, prayers, support, encouragement, phone calls, birthday/anniversary greetings and connection continue even now as we have pastored for 6 years. You've guided, served, wept and rejoiced with us throughout these pivotal moments in our lives despite your personal seasons of loss and grief. The extension of grace and ability to maintain an eternal focus even when facing obstacles is quite remarkable. We are grateful for the intersection of our lives and will forever be changed by the faithfulness of God through you, His faithful servant."

- **Reflect:** In what areas do you notice your leader needs ministering? Are there particular times or situations in which he tends to be weaker and in greater need of ministry?

- **Receive:** *The generous will prosper; those who refresh others will themselves be refreshed.* (Proverbs 11:25, NLT)

- **Respond:** Thank God you are in position to minister to your leader. Set a reminder to purposefully reach out to him on occasion, that you may impart strength and encouragement. Be aware of the leading of the Holy Spirit, Who may direct you to ministry when it is most needed.

MY REFLECTIONS

CHAPTER 12

DO YOU KEEP YOUR HEART RIGHT?

A little leaven leavens the whole lump.
(Galatians 5:9)

LITTLE things matter. Let's look at some examples.

It took nearly 2,500 years to build the Great Wall of China. There certainly are plenty of myths surrounding this remarkable feat of human achievement. It is said that on at least one section of the wall, the builder required any soil used in construction to be gathered from a minimum depth of two feet below the surface. This would ensure no seeds from the fertile topsoil would germinate later and cause structural issues within the wall. Whether or not this was true, it certainly makes sense. As plenty of homeowners can attest, a tiny seed that establishes sufficient root can, over the course of many years, destroy a concrete driveway as it matures into a full-grown tree. Speaking of seeds, Jesus had something to say about them in Mark 4:30-32, when He talked about how tiny a mustard seed is. We all know from that parable how large it is when it is fully grown!

We could go further and consider something even smaller than a mustard seed. The National Museum of Civil War Medicine says:

> "Disease was responsible for two-thirds of all Civil War deaths. Tragically, if we had only known about germ theory, so many deaths could have been prevented."[1]

In other words, the brutal gauntlet of battles, bullets, and bayonets of the American Civil War are not what killed most of our soldiers. Something much smaller did – disease-causing germs. It did not take a serious battle injury to bring down our finest. Tiny germs introduced during a post-battle surgery, coupled with the lack of medical knowledge and lack of antiseptic protocols during that time period, took them out left and right.

As I am writing this chapter, I am currently preaching a series at Life Church Smyrna entitled "Small Things." Each message serves to focus our attention on the fact that even small things can have a significant impact on our lives and the lives of others. (If you are interested, you can find those messages at: LifeChurchSmyrna.com, on our Facebook page, or on our YouTube channel.)

> We need to mind ourselves when it comes to integrity.

The phenomenon of little things having such a huge impact changed the course of the life of meteorologist Edward Lorenz. He published a seminal paper in 1972 that asked the seemingly absurd question, "Does the Flap of a Butterfly's Wings in Brazil Set Off a Tornado in Texas?"[2] At first glance it seems impossible, yet he coined the term 'butterfly effect' to describe how over time or during the modeling of a complicated weather forecast, the tiniest, seemingly most inconsequential occurrences can turn a sunny afternoon into a deadly storm.

Why the examples on little things? Because there's a little thing called integrity. We need to mind ourselves when it comes to integrity. My working definition for integrity is: "Doing the right thing even when nobody else is looking," but it really means much more. In my opinion, there are few things more important for a secondary leader than integrity. Zig Ziglar said:

> "It is true that integrity alone won't make you a leader, but without integrity you will never be one."[3]

You might acquire a title and you might have a lot of people reporting to you, but you cannot be a leader in the truest sense of the word without integrity. Like a mustard seed, integrity starts out as a small thing that grows into something else. It will, in many ways, determine the trajectory of your life.

Jesus said in Luke 16:10, *If we are faithful in little things, we will also be faithful with much. Likewise, if we are unjust in little things, we also will be unjust in greater things.* I think we all know what it means to be faithful, but let's look carefully at the word translated as "unjust." This word is used in various places in scripture and has meanings far beyond a simple lack of justice; it refers to someone who is unrighteous. It describes someone who deals fraudulently with others. Does that sound like someone you want on the staff? Would you want such an individual to influence your leader? Maybe integrity isn't a small thing after all –

maybe it's downright huge!

This is another clear example of how the world's system is backwards. Too many people think nothing of telling a white lie – it's such a little thing, right? That attitude can then progress to making unethical decisions in the organization with the justification of, "that's just business," as if God should not have a say in what we do during business meetings. If we think we can carve out such a niche in the boardroom, then it's a very short drive from there to say that "what happens in the bedroom is my own business." Such is the worldly path when what appears to be a very small violation of integrity grows into something far worse. Those small, deceptive seeds we plant do not magically improve themselves over time and morph into a harvest of righteousness and integrity. This is a spiritual truth, not just a practical one, as we find in Galatians 6:7: *Do not be deceived, God is not mocked; for whatever a man sows, that he will also reap.*

> It's never right to do the wrong thing, it's never wrong to do the right thing, it's always right to do the right thing and it's always wrong to do the wrong thing.

The lesson to each of us is clear – we must guard our hearts, as Proverbs 4:23 wisely cautions. We must work steadily and diligently to keep our hearts right. This is true for all believers, but doubly critical for leaders. James 3:1 instructs that not everyone should desire to be a teacher (e.g., a leader), as teachers will be judged by a higher standard. It is not only a matter of God judging us – the members of our congregation or our business will rightly hold us to a higher standard by virtue of our positions.

The higher up you go, the greater the standard to which you will be held. A comment made by a parking lot attendant might not raise any eyebrows, but that same comment could be considered unacceptable if said by the senior leader. As godly leaders, our standards should remain high and above reproach. We may not use that word much today, but centuries ago it meant one was above censure or rebuke.

This brings to mind Galatians 5:23, where we find the fruit of the Spirit: love, joy, peace, patience, kindness, goodness, faithfulness, gentleness, and self-control. Observe what it says about this fruit: *against such things there is no law.* In other words, one cannot be censured because she demonstrates an abundance of love. One cannot be rebuked for his faithfulness. It just is not possible to do so with a straight face!

When our son S.J. was young (about kindergarten age) he and I were talking about a situation that happened at school. Something another boy did troubled him, because he knew the boy's actions were wrong. In trying to help him, I attempted to keep the communication on a level he could understand. Although I do not remember all the details of our conversation, I clearly remember saying this phrase: "S.J., it's never right to do the wrong thing." Over the next few years, S.J. would extend that thought and say, "Dad, it's never right to do the wrong thing, it's never wrong to do the right thing, it's always right to do the right thing and it's always wrong to do the wrong thing." Even though those phrases are simplistic, it helped me to know he was listening and learning the importance of integrity.

One of the greatest honors in my life was working alongside my Dad in the furniture and appliance business he owned. I was in my early twenties; my Dad was (and still is) my hero. During that time, he taught me so much about how to run a business. He did so simply by example. I recall one time when a lady was shopping for a particular double oven that was quite expensive. She had gotten prices from other appliance dealers, so Dad knew he only had one chance to close this deal. His price had to be lower than everyone else's. This was not an item we stocked, so Dad called the manufacturer to find out what he would pay, calculated his profit margin, and gave the lady a price. She accepted the deal and paid for the appliance. Several days passed and Dad called her when the item had been received to set up delivery and installation. What he did next will forever stand out in my mind as one of the greatest lessons in integrity.

I can almost remember the phone conversation, which went something like this:

> The higher up you go, the greater the standard to which you will be held. A comment made by a parking lot attendant might not raise any eyebrows, but that same comment could be considered unacceptable if said by the senior leader.

"Good morning. This is Billy Osbon at Garvan Furniture and Appliance. I wanted to let you know your oven has arrived. Yes, we can deliver it tomorrow. Oh, and by the way, I will be sending you a check for $100.00 when they bring your oven. Why? Well, you see, I gave you a fair price based on what it was supposed to cost me. But, when the item arrived, I noticed that GE was running a promotion and it cost me $100.00 less than I was originally told. So, you see, my savings is your savings, which is why I will be sending that check with the delivery guys."

The lady was blown away. She said she could not believe Dad had not just kept the money for himself! I believe he did not keep the money because my Dad understood the importance of integrity — even when nobody else is looking. Thanks, Dad, for teaching me that it's never right to do the wrong thing.

So, what does this mean for us? In practical terms, what can we do to "guard our hearts" and purposefully work to keep our hearts right? As you might have guessed, it starts with the small things, particularly in your speech right down to your choice of words:

- Choose speech which indicates your desire to do the right thing, rather than what is convenient or politically expedient.

- Maintain clean speech, as coarse joking and profanity will lower your standing in the eyes of others.

- Avoid gossip and refuse to be drawn into contentious discussions, which are unfruitful.

- Live and act in such a way that it is clear to others your moral and ethical standards are non-negotiable.

- Exercise care and wisdom in private meetings and other interactions with the opposite sex.

- The standard for leaders is not that you merely be innocent of serious wrongdoing, but that you are above reproach.

Above all, understand a life of integrity does not occur in a vacuum — it absolutely is a conscious choice each of us must make. We must make it in light of the ultimate standard, which is the infallible, inerrant Word of God. That is no small thing.

- **Reflect:** Is there an area in your life in which you struggle with integrity? If so, what small steps can you make today to deal with it?

- **Receive:** *To do what is right and just is more acceptable to the Lord than sacrifice.* (Proverbs 21:3, NIV)

- **Respond:** This week, keep a close eye on your words, your thoughts, your actions, and your motives. Resolve to make any necessary changes, so that you, indeed, will be called "above reproach."

MY REFLECTIONS

CHAPTER 13

WILL YOU SERVE WITH EXCELLENCE?

Slack habits and sloppy work are as bad as vandalism.
(Proverbs 18:9, MSG)

AUTHOR and motivational expert James Clear once talked about the fascinating and phenomenal turnaround of the British Cycling team.[1] A century ago, they languished at the bottom of the proverbial barrel in their sport. They were considered pretty much a joke. In nearly a hundred years, they had exactly one Olympic gold medal to their credit. At the Tour de France (cycling's biggest event) they had never even had a win. It was so bad that one of the most elite bike manufacturers in all of Europe refused to sell them any of their bikes. The manufacturer reasoned that their sales and reputation could be harmed if people looked at the British Team and noted what brand of bikes they used during their endless losses. I could not imagine much more of a humiliating rejection. How do you even begin to fix such a colossal mess?

The world discovered the answer in 2003 when the team hired a new coach. He employed a strategy of taking every single thing that could conceivably impact the team's performance and sought to improve it by 1%. Every. Single. Thing. Sure, they looked at the obvious stuff and made some changes. More significantly, they put everything under the microscope to see how it could be made just a little better. They found certain fabrics to be lighter and more aerodynamic, so they switched their uniform fabrics. They painted the inside of the equipment truck white to better spot any dust that might degrade the performance of their bikes. They made literally hundreds of other tiny improvements. No area was deemed too small or inconsequential to ignore.

The results were beyond shocking. It took only five short years for the British Cycling team to dominate their events at the Olympics. By 2017 they had racked up an astounding sixty-six Olympic or Paralympic gold medals. The annual Tour de France? Five wins within a six-year period. History was re-written, and the British Cycling team became the stuff of legends. I would imagine no one would have any problems selling them a bike!

Now, let's make this all about you. God's Word does not just teach us to pray, love others, and be faithful. It also focuses very heavily on the concept of excellence. The question for today is: Will you serve with excellence?

Consider the Word of the Lord in Numbers chapter 3, verses 5-9: *And the Lord spoke to Moses, saying: "Bring the tribe of Levi near, and present them before Aaron the priest, that they may serve him. And they shall attend to his needs and the needs of the whole congregation before the tabernacle of meeting, to do the work of the tabernacle. Also, they shall attend to all the furnishings of the tabernacle of meeting, and to the*

> God's Word does not just teach us to pray, love others, and be faithful. It also focuses very heavily on the concept of excellence.

needs of the children of Israel, to do the work of the tabernacle. And you shall give the Levites to Aaron and his sons; they are given entirely to him from among the children of Israel."

This passage does not merely point out that the Levites were to work for Aaron and the congregation. It also alludes to the fact that Aaron needed to be able to rely upon these secondary leaders to do their work with excellence...even down to matters seemingly as inconsequential as the furnishings of the tabernacle. We must ask ourselves if God made such a specific request, there must have been an extraordinarily important reason for Him to do so. To interpret scripture any other way would be to believe that God asks us to waste valuable time and scarce resources on unimportant things. Does God's Word focus on excellence? Let us look at just a few examples:

- Daniel 6:3: *Daniel distinguished himself above the governors and satraps, because an excellent spirit was in him; and the king gave thought to setting him over the whole realm.*

- Matthew 5:16: *Let your light so shine before men, that they may see your good works and glorify your Father in heaven.*

- 1 Corinthians 12:31: *But earnestly desire the best gifts. And yet I show you a more excellent way.*

- 2 Corinthians 8:7: *But as you abound in everything – in faith, in speech, in knowledge, in all diligence, and in your love for us – see that you abound in this grace also.*

- Philippians 1:9-10: *And it is my prayer that your love may abound more and more, with knowledge and all discernment, so that you may approve what is excellent, and so be pure and blameless for the day of Christ."*

- Philippians 4:8: *Finally, brothers, whatever is true, whatever is honorable, whatever is just, whatever is pure, whatever is lovely, whatever is commendable, if there is any excellence, if there is anything worthy of praise, think about these things.*

- Colossians 3:23: *And whatever you do, do it heartily, as to the Lord and not to men.*

- Titus 2:7: *In all things showing yourself to be a pattern of good works; in doctrine showing integrity, reverence, incorruptibility.*

It seems we can learn a lesson here: What God does, He always does with excellence. He did not leave a stone unturned; He did not spare an expense; He did not do things halfway. We who invest our lives in the service of the kingdom should therefore resolve to do our jobs with excellence.

Notice within each of these passages there are one or more words which directly emphasize the need for excellence. Pay particular attention to phrases such as "do it heartily;" "in all diligence;" and "a pattern of good works." It is very clear our Lord does not want us to serve half-heartedly. He showed us through His sacrificial life that giving our all is what it takes to serve with excellence.

I like how Daniel is said to have had an excellent spirit. King Belshazzar threw a lavish banquet, and during the feast, a cryptic

> Always be ready and willing to serve. Even if you're not scheduled to serve, be willing to step in when you are genuinely needed.

message supernaturally appeared, which terrified him. The queen came to him and recommended that Daniel be summoned, saying, *"Inasmuch as an excellent spirit, knowledge, understanding, interpreting dreams, solving riddles, and explaining enigmas were found in this Daniel, whom the king named Belteshazzar, now let Daniel be called, and he will give the interpretation."*

From the queen's description, there seems to be very little about Daniel's approach to life that was ordinary. For that matter, there is nothing about Christ's approach that was ordinary. I would be hard-pressed to think of a single thing Christ did which was not done in excellence. Shouldn't we follow His example? It seems we can learn a lesson here: What God does, He always does with excellence. He did not leave a stone unturned; He did not spare an expense; He did not do things halfway. We who invest our lives in the service of the kingdom should therefore resolve to do our jobs with excellence.

Even during the preparation for services and even during the little things within the organization, you will see it is very common for senior leaders to demand excellence. The intent is not to be picky. It is certainly not to come across as requiring everyone to conform to the personal preferences of a single leader. The heart behind this is to honor both God and man.

During our services, for example, we consider that fundamentally, we want an audience with the King. Would we be picky about how we clean our houses if we were preparing for a royal visit? Would we not pressure wash the driveway, plant new flowers, put every scrap of trash away, and possibly even buy a new outfit for the occasion? How much more so for an audience with God? We also strive for excellence during the program to honor those who are present in the congregation or watching the sermon online. The intent is not to have "worship-tainment" and wow them with sound effects and technology. We do, however, want them to see that we have not taken our jobs lightly and have been diligent to have a solid plan and a smooth execution to the best of our abilities.

For the nearly nineteen years I have been privileged to serve as Lead Pastor of Life Church Smyrna, my constant mantra with the team has been:

"We can do better, and we will do better."

They have heard this countless times when we were assessing a large event, community outreach or even one of our weekly services. The admission is two-fold: (1) nothing was perfect and (2) some things can be improved.

Excellent secondary leaders are easy to spot, even if everyone cannot agree on exactly what makes them so excellent. There often is a quiet, very deep respect which people have for them as they witness their incredible faithfulness and diligence year after year. There may not be many awards banquets where their achievements are lauded, but ask long-time members of the organizations how things get done. They will not pause in naming some of the secondary leaders who consistently go above and beyond. Serving with excellence means you follow the counsel of Matthew 5:41 in both letter and spirit: *And whoever compels you to go one mile, go with him two.* What does this look like in practice?

- Always be ready and willing to serve. Even if you're not scheduled to serve, be willing to step in when you are genuinely needed. Even if it is not your primary area of service, and even if you don't necessarily feel that you're good at a particular task, be willing to serve.

- Be quick to smile and quick to encourage others. Some of the people who walk through your doors are on their last leg before they give up completely. Be a reason and an inspiration for them to keep on going.

- Actively look for small ways to make things better, for small changes add up to real changes over time.

- Look for ways to support other secondary leaders. We are a team, and our collective load becomes lighter when each of us looks out for the others.

- Refuse to cut corners. When something is deemed to be "good enough," put a bit more work into it.

God is honored by excellence. That truth alone should impact the way we approach our jobs, our level of service, and so much more. What a privilege! What a responsibility!

- **Reflect:** What area in your life would you say is most marked by excellence? What area in your life needs the most improvement?

- **Receive:** 1 Corinthians 10:31: *Therefore, whether you eat or drink, or whatever you do, do all to the glory of God.*

- **Respond:** Using the same principles of the British Cycling Team, what tiny, seemingly inconsequential changes can you make today that collectively would result in a higher level of excellence in your life?

MY REFLECTIONS

CHAPTER 14

WILL YOU ACTIVELY WORK FOR UNITY?

Behold, how good and how pleasant it is for brethren to dwell together in unity!
(Psalm 133:1)

"**J**OIN or die." That kind of slogan doesn't give you a warm fuzzy feeling, does it? Imagine if your senior leader were to adopt such an attitude to inspire support for a new initiative! In 1754, that slogan is exactly what Benjamin Franklin used in a valiant attempt to unite the colonies against an external threat. He even published a rather morbid meme: a snake cut up into many pieces with each piece symbolizing a separate, disunified colony. Well over two hundred years before the modern word *meme* was coined, Franklin not only used one...it became the first political image to go viral in America.[1]

There is a second line also attributed to this American founding father, allegedly made at the signing of the Declaration of Independence:

> "We must all hang together, or, most assuredly, we shall all hang separately."

In other words, those who put their names on that famous document knew if they did not band together and succeed in the war for independence, the British would execute them (probably by hanging each of them).

I open this chapter with such stark analogies for a very good reason: to illustrate how critical it is for us to work for unity within our organization. It is not an exaggeration to say if we as leaders do not band together and work for unity, we one day will see the organization destroyed. I cannot afford to mince words on this subject. Just like in the days of the

American Revolution, this is war. A cruel, merciless enemy far more deadly than the British has risen against us. He would love to see us annihilated.

Unity. Harmony. Peace. A team working together toward a common, worthy goal. These are beautiful words, aren't they? Parents with multiple children know the blessed peace that results when their children get along and play together without bickering and complaining because Johnny has all the red LEGOs. How much more is God pleased when we honor Him by living in harmony with

> Unity is not an event, an annual sermon, or an occasional emphasis. It is an integral, ongoing part of an organization's success. Over the long term, we will not succeed without it.

others who are made in His image? No wonder the psalmist expressed so eloquently in Psalm 133:1: *How wonderful, how beautiful, when brothers and sisters get along!* (MSG)

The focus for today is unity. It is something we inherently understand we need, but often fail to work toward. That is why the title includes the key word "actively." Will you actively work for the unity of your organization? Unity is not an event, an annual sermon, or an occasional emphasis. It is an integral, ongoing part of an organization's success. Over the long term, we will not succeed without it. With that said, there are four key areas on which we need to focus when it comes to unity within our organization: Unity with the primary leader, unity with staff and other secondary leaders, unity within the organization, and unity in doctrinal matters and corporate direction.

- **Unity with the primary leader**

I think we all want to have a great relationship with our boss. It makes the workday go smoother and is one way to keep our stress levels in check. If only a great relationship happened automatically! It takes continual effort by both parties to make any relationship thrive. Speaking from the standpoint of a wise secondary leader, we should endeavor to understand more about our primary leader. There is great wisdom in investing genuine effort to understand what the primary leader is doing and why he is doing it. Most leaders do not operate in a vacuum. There are a dizzying array of forces, decisions, obstacles, and goals that come together to influence what the leader can accomplish. As we note elsewhere in this work, much of it is behind the scenes and not visible.

The wise secondary leader will attempt to understand more about what drives the leader and what he is attempting to accomplish. In doing so, it is easier to increase a rapport with the senior leader and simultaneously build stronger unity.

We can work for unity with our primary leader by embracing a concept known as "seeking first to understand." That phrase may sound familiar, particularly if you have read Dr. Stephen R. Covey's book, *The Seven Habits of Highly Effective People*. This was a particularly important lesson and Dr. Covey went so far as to say:

> "If I were to summarize in one sentence the single most important principle I have learned in the field of interpersonal relations, it would be this: Seek first to understand, then to be understood."[2]

> **Resolve to have absolutely nothing to do with any attack on your leader, and resolve to be gentle (but vocal) in communicating to others that you will not join any such attack.**

He goes on to explain how most people listen to others not so much to understand the other person, but to offer a reply.

You probably know someone who excels at that. You can tell they are not truly listening to you, but are only waiting for a chance to open their mouth again and tell you what they think. It is frustrating to work with someone like that. Deep down, you know you are not getting through to them. They are not opening themselves up to true communication and are not likely to be receptive to any real change that's needed.

One of the best examples on this topic can be found in Proverbs 18:13: *It's stupid and embarrassing to give an answer before you listen.* (CEV) The reality is we oftentimes end up looking stupid and embarrassing ourselves when we don't take time to listen to our primary leader. It is so easy to become fixated on talking that we end up not listening.

James Dent once quipped,

> "As you go through life, you are going to have many opportunities to keep your mouth shut. Take advantage of all of them."[3]

When your primary leader speaks, do your very best to hear the heart behind the words. What is the senior leader trying to do that goes beyond the present conversation? Where does he spend his time? What motivates him? What special gifts has God given him? Identifying those gifts can be a direct and powerful indication of how God wants to use him. The more you understand what your leader is all about, the greater unity you can build by supporting it.

Never underestimate the power of unity within an organization, especially as it pertains to the primary leader. How the enemy loves to take down a primary leader! Do you remember the "Mayhem" commercials Allstate ran some time ago? While the commercials were quite humorous, creating total mayhem is precisely what the enemy wants to do within your organization. Even if he fails in destroying a leader outright, sometimes he can create enough mayhem to distract the leader from focusing on what God wants to do. A leader sidelined by distractions is an ineffective leader, and the enemy knows that very well. Resolve to have absolutely nothing to do with any attack on your leader, and resolve to be gentle (but vocal) in communicating to others that you will not join any such attack.

You must fight for unity. A couple members of our congregation previously attended Church at Chapel Hill under the leadership of Pastor Dave Divine. (How's that for a cool name for a senior pastor!) At an introductory membership dinner, they recalled how Pastor Dave talked about unity. This wonderful man of God is not at all physically intimidating, but they recall how he looked like a warrior when he said to the assembled group: "I will fight for unity." In other words, there were some areas in which his leadership style might be laid back. On any matter threatening unity within the organization, he would come out fighting with everything he had, every time. Adopt that same attitude when it comes to your primary leader.

- **Unity with staff and other secondary leaders**

Be sober, be vigilant; because your adversary the devil walks about like a roaring lion, seeking whom he may devour. (1 Peter 5:8) These vivid words are always relevant for us when it comes to how we interact with other leaders within our organization.

In the wild, it is a common tactic for predators to try to separate a herd. It is far easier to pick off a lone, weaker individual than it is to successfully attack a larger group. Attacking a unified herd head-on can be deadly; even a powerful apex predator risks being trampled to death by a herd of strong animals bound and determined to protect their young. A predator will ordinarily not even make such an attempt.

We are wise to be on the lookout for that tactic when it comes to remaining in close unity with other leaders within our organization. We know from 1 Peter 5:8 that our adversary is always looking for an opening (some means to infiltrate) and we bind together in godly harmony to resist any effort to disrupt our unity.

In Ephesians chapter 6, the Apostle Paul stresses the significance of unity and identifying our enemy by using the analogy of a soldier going into battle. He writes: *A final word: Be strong in the Lord and in his mighty power. Put on all of God's armor so that you will be able to stand firm against all strategies of the devil. For we are not fighting against flesh-and-blood enemies, but against evil rulers and authorities of the unseen world, against mighty powers in this dark world, and against evil spirits in the heavenly places.* (Ephesians 6:10-12) As followers of Christ, it should be crystal clear to us that our enemy is not another staff member, another church or another organization. Our enemy is God's enemy.

Paul continues by encouraging the church to get dressed for battle as he writes: *Therefore, put on every piece of God's armor so you will be able to resist the enemy in the time of evil. Then after the battle you will still be standing firm. Stand your ground, putting on the belt of truth and the body armor of God's righteousness. For shoes, put on the peace that comes from the Good News so that you will be fully prepared. In addition to all of these, hold up the shield of faith to stop the fiery arrows of the devil. Put on salvation as your helmet, and take the sword of the Spirit, which is the word of God. Pray in the Spirit at all times and on every occasion. Stay alert and be persistent in your prayers for all believers everywhere.* (Ephesians 6:13-18)

> You must fight for unity.

While every part of the armor of God is essential, for this chapter I want to focus on the shield of faith. Paul says this essential piece of armor can stop the fiery arrows of the devil. The reference is a powerful one when we understand the context of Paul's era. A Roman battle shield was called the scutum. It was long, square shaped and decorated. It covered about three-quarters of a man's body and was sturdy enough to serve as a stretcher for the dead and wounded soldiers who would have to be carried off the battlefield.

> Never underestimate the power of unity within an organization, especially as it pertains to the primary leader.

In times of combat, Roman soldiers would link their shields together and stand in a line shoulder-to-shoulder. In this way, not just one soldier, but all had a metal wall in front of them to protect them from the onslaught of their enemy. A single shield was of some use in knocking down a single foe, but the real power was found when they were locked together in unity. This is an interesting metaphor for every organization: we are more powerful working in harmony than as individuals.

Many of you may remember the Three Musketeers who famously cried, "All for one, one for all" as their outward sign of unity. They were committed to the task before them because they were committed to the other men beside them. This is the essence of unity. This is the essence of victory.

We can work with other staff members and secondary leaders in several ways. First, we remember Whose team we are on. It is not about our personal agendas, not even the agenda of the primary leader. We serve God as members of one body, and it helps to remember this when we relate to other leaders within our organization. Remembering Whose team we are on helps us to put aside any differences as we work toward common goals.

Second, we must understand the enemy doesn't just want to destroy some other leader six offices down who is going through a particularly difficult time (perhaps even of his own making). I am sure you love everyone on staff, but even if that person happens to be your least favorite, understand the enemy's ultimate goal is not to bring down that one individual. The enemy wants to drive wedges between us so he can divide and conquer.

Solomon wrote on the power of unity in Ecclesiastes 4:9-12: *Two people are better off than one, for they can help each other succeed. If one person falls, the other can reach out and help. But someone who falls alone is in real trouble. Likewise, two people lying close together can keep each other warm. But how can one be warm alone? A person standing alone can be attacked and defeated, but two can stand back-to-back and conquer. Three are even better, for a triple-braided cord is not easily broken.*

Returning to our earlier analogy from the wild, the predator sees an injured animal trying valiantly to keep up with the rest of the herd, but not quite making it. He knows he has just spotted his next meal, so he moves in quickly to attack. If the injured animal were not so isolated, he would not be such an easy target.

Once the enemy finishes with one member of your team, guess who is next? At some point, the enemy will focus a targeted attack on you. Without that other guy fighting for you in your time of need, you will not have the same prayer covering. He needs you, and you need him.

Third, let us understand many attacks on unity have the appearance of legitimacy. It may not even look like an attack. If we do not remain constantly on guard, we may unwittingly fall into a trap that a very cunning enemy has set for us. Matthew 10:16 cautions us as believers in this regard: *Behold, I send you out as sheep in the midst of wolves. Therefore, be wise as serpents and harmless as doves.*

> We know from 1 Peter 5:8 that our adversary is always looking for an opening (some means to infiltrate) and we bind together in godly harmony to resist any effort to disrupt our unity.

If someone approaches you and baits you with gossip or slander, however elegant and well-intended it may seem, immediately raise your guard. Consider not only the other person's motives, but also your own in choosing to participate in the conversation. Is this an attempt to cause division? Is the charge true? Even so, is this the proper channel or the proper way it should be handled?

It is always correct to actively seek the guidance and the wisdom of the Holy Spirit in such a situation. We can be tricked, but the Holy Spirit not only sees right through the endless schemes of the enemy, but He also knows exactly how to disarm the enemy as well as how to effectively counterattack.

On that note, we as leaders, need to maintain a strong, disciplined prayer life. We need to ask God how we can pray for other leaders in the organization and how we can partner with them so that God can use our combined talents to create synergies that not only strengthen our unity, but also make our jobs more fun.

Understand the best result of a targeted attack by our enemy is not that the attack fails. The best result is that such an attack backfires royally in the face of the enemy and causes God's kingdom to grow. There is nothing like watching the enemy flee while the people of God rejoice!

- Unity within the organization

1 Corinthians 12:12 and 14 remind us: *The human body has many parts, but the many parts make up one whole body. So it is with the body of Christ...Yes, the body has many different parts, not just one part.* (NLT)

Within the church, it is almost expected to have an annual sermon on the topic of unity within the organization. The purpose is to bring the congregation together and remind ourselves of how much we need each other. Indeed, it makes for a great sermon, but it is not a mere rite of passage, an easy message for the preacher to repeat. Congregations are living, dynamic entities. There is always much going on behind the scenes.

If someone approaches you and baits you with gossip or slander, however elegant and well-intended it may seem, immediately raise your guard. Consider not only the other person's motives, but also your own in choosing to participate in the conversation.

Some families are going through excruciating trials. New members introduce new group dynamics. Changing leadership makes people nervous about losing the status quo. These and a dozen other components come together to create constant tension. We cannot keep everything the same year after year, but neither do we want to change so much that we grow apart and lose the things about our organization that drew us there in the first place. Through it all, we each have hope we will not only remain together, but grow closer during the process.

In support of this goal, we can work actively to ensure our interactions within our organizations are in this same spirit of unity. Extending common courtesies and showing simple respect go such a long way in this regard. We do not need to be naïve in thinking we will always be around the proverbial campfire singing "Kumbaya" and enjoying perfect unity with others. Sometimes people will rub us the wrong way and sometimes we will miss the mark, too. In fact, as I have often said, some folks will get on your reserve nerve! We will not always bat a thousand, but we can do our best to treat each other well and to honor the feelings of others even when we do not necessarily agree with a particular viewpoint.

Speaking of viewpoints, let me encourage you to go out of your way to avoid contentious political discussions, not only in person but also on social media. This seems to be even more necessary at this time than at any other time that I can remember. We can work with people from around the world, we can live next door to someone from another country and we can even attend a multi-cultural church, but that does not mean we vote the same way. It may be a small world, but it's not so small that everyone is the same.

Keep that in mind when posting on social media, especially as leaders within an organization. Caustic, polarizing comments have no place on our walls! It may well be your rightful opinion, but as a team member, you have a greater responsibility than most in choosing the content on your social media platforms. May we be gently reminded of the description of the believers in Acts 4:32: *All the believers were one in heart and mind. No one claimed that any of their possessions was their own, but they shared everything they had.* They did not even claim their possessions as their own. How infinitely better the social media world would be if we would adopt such an attitude and think before we post!

- Unity in doctrinal matters and corporate direction

Unfortunately, church history has been littered with internal wars, divisions, splits, and strife. Of course, the same can be true within the realms of any other organization, as these dynamics are related to people who comprise churches, businesses, government, etc. This is hardly the picture of living in unity as we noted earlier in Psalm 133:1, is it?

Case in point: if you want to find out how many denominations exist just within Protestantism, good luck. Numbers vary wildly from one hundred and eighty to as many as forty-seven thousand! While some began peacefully and under the Lord's direction, others were the result of ugly, messy splits among people who lost sight of the mandate of unity.

The problem in many cases is that when a doctrinal matter arises, too often we find ourselves pushing for an interpretation that matches our personal opinions, choices, or preferences. Let us take a step back for a moment. Even when considering the latest hot-

> We can work for unity on matters of doctrine and corporate direction by submitting to God's Word at every turn. We must seek the perfect counsel of the Holy Spirit in every matter of unity.

button topic that threatens to polarize the community, whose opinion really matters? At least on some level, my opinion does not matter... and neither does yours! What matters is God's Word, which does not change with the tide of public opinion or the rise and fall of various political factions. It must be our standard for living in a world that is constantly changing.

Consider James 1:17 which says: *Every good gift and every perfect gift is from above, and comes down from the Father of lights, with Whom there is no variation or shadow of turning.* A shadow occurs when light is partially blocked from a source. When we consider that God is the perfect source of light, it is not possible for there to be a shadow around God.

When we read about being "in the shadow of the Almighty," it refers to being in the presence of God. Hebrews 13:8 speaks the truth about Christ Jesus, that He: *is the same yesterday, today, and forever.* That refers to His character, His nature, and His divine position on any given topic. It simply does not change, and our job is to align ourselves with His Word. That needs to happen both individually and corporately, but it must begin individually. Unity is a personal choice.

We can work for unity on matters of doctrine and corporate direction by submitting to God's Word at every turn. We must seek the perfect counsel of the Holy Spirit in every matter of unity. There certainly are times where sincere, mature believers will have a different point of view, but we are to remember the sacred bonds of unity whenever we are in a potentially contentious situation. Our personal preferences do not justify strife within the church or the organization. Only when others are trying to advance a doctrine or direction which clearly opposes God's Word should we be willing to break ranks.

Unity is worth fighting for and it starts with us.

> Even when considering the latest hot-button topic that threatens to polarize the community, whose opinion really matters? At least on some level, my opinion does not matter... and neither does yours!

- **Reflect:** What are a few areas where you personally can work to advance the cause of unity within the organization? Is there any area in which you could be causing disunity?

- **Receive:** Romans 14:19: *Let us therefore make every effort to do what leads to peace and to mutual edification.*

- **Respond:** Remember that unity is partly an action word – it is not merely a state describing the condition or quality of our interactions with others but something on which we must actively maintain. Resolve to do your part to keep the bonds of unity strong.

MY REFLECTIONS

CHAPTER 15

DO YOU UNDERSTAND THE VALUE OF MENTORING?

You have heard me teach things that have been confirmed
by many reliable witnesses. Now teach these truths to other trustworthy
people who will be able to pass them on to others.
(2 Timothy 2:2)

THE four phases of mentoring are defined as:

- **Preparing**: When you find out if mentorship is right for you.

- **Negotiating**: When you help your mentee set learning goals.

- **Enabling growth**: When you support and provide feedback to your mentee.

- **Coming to closure**: Where you assess the value of your mentoring relationship and move forward.

We would do well to keep these phases in mind as we endeavor to be a mentor or to seek out a mentor. The value of the mentoring relationship will reflect in how well each of these four phases are completed. Over time, the mentor and the mentee should both develop their life skills to continue with the maturation process each ultimately desires to achieve.

Hans Finzel says today's leaders have five problems:

- They replicate the poor leadership skills of others,

- They lack basic skills for leadership,

- They lack good mentors,

- They lack formal leadership training, and

- They are unable to distinguish between secular and Biblical leadership values. [1]

Did you notice the problem of not having a good mentor is sandwiched right in the middle of the other problems? It might well be said that mentoring, or the lack thereof, is at the center or the core of the issues facing leaders today and that good mentoring could potentially solve many of those same problems.

Mentoring is an underestimated art. Some of the most successful educational and leadership programs understand its enormous value. Classical Conversations is one such organization, the local chapter of which has met in our facility for many years. Promoting a high-quality, Christ-centered homeschooling experience, one of the goals is for high school seniors to learn the material so well and develop presentation skills to the point they are comfortable teaching certain elements to younger students.

West Point Academy, our nation's premiere military school, has long adopted a similar approach. Incoming freshmen, called cadets, are first taught leadership by learning how to follow. As they progress in their studies, they take on increasingly significant leadership responsibilities. This culminates in their own ability to influence younger cadets and have a real hand in guiding them.

The four phases of mentoring are defined as:

- **Preparing:** When you find out if mentorship is right for you.

- **Negotiating:** When you help your mentee set learning goals.

- **Enabling growth:** When you support and provide feedback to your mentee.

- **Coming to closure:** Where you assess the value of your mentoring relationship and move forward.

> Like every good mentor, Jesus not only affirmed the positive attributes in their lives, but He also challenged the negative attributes. He desired them to be the very best people possible, and He knew His teachings would enable them to reach that goal.

The school takes it even further if a cadet commits a "discretion" or violation of the Academy's code. Such cadets may be placed in the U.S. Military Academy's "Honor Mentorship Program" which is an intensive six-month process designed to help the cadet learn from his or her mistake and grow from it. The Academy expends very serious resources on this because one of its core principles is to build the strongest levels of honor and character among its graduates. This helps prepare them for even greater challenges ahead.

Even more importantly, many examples of mentorship are found throughout Scripture. A careful study of the Bible will demonstrate how such interactions literally changed the course of history, time and time again. Even though the term "mentor" does not formally appear in Scripture, clear examples abound. Remember how Jethro taught Moses about leadership in Exodus chapter 18? He explained the value of appointing judges, so Moses did not have to personally handle the nonstop flood of complaints and civil cases brought before him from morning until evening. Such a move not only freed up Moses to handle far more important matters and more effectively guide the nation, it also likely prevented him from burning out and giving up altogether.

What would history have been like if Moses' influence had been cut short? It most certainly did not stop there, for Moses subsequently mentored Joshua. Joshua would one day take over the gargantuan task of leading such an obstinate people as the Israelites. Joshua, in turn, would go on to train many leaders in his army. To say that these successive mentorships affected political and military history is an understatement.

On the spiritual front, consider how Eli taught Samuel through mentoring. Samuel mentored David who, without a doubt, became Israel's greatest king. David in turn mentored his son, Solomon, who became the wisest king ever to live. Solomon mentored the visiting Queen of Sheba, who returned to her own land with newfound wisdom. This turn of events spread godly wisdom and influence probably far beyond anything Eli ever conceived! Such is often the cascading and unstoppable impact of mentoring, so any work with secondary leadership must include this crucial element of leadership development.

We certainly cannot overlook that Jesus mentored the disciples, as well. From the beginning of His earthly ministry, Jesus took time to model the leadership principles and life skills He desired these men to exemplify. As they walked together for those three-and-a-half years, Jesus took the time to personally teach them truths that would shape their destinies as well as those they would eventually lead. Like every good mentor, Jesus not only affirmed the positive attributes in their lives, but He also challenged the negative attributes. He desired them to be the very best people possible, and He knew His teachings would enable them to reach that goal.

In the beginning, Jesus did everything and the disciples watched. As time went on, Jesus and the disciples worked together. In the end, Jesus left, and the disciples carried on the work He began. That sounds like the epitome of mentoring to me, as the end result of how we lead others is to ensure the work continues long after we are gone. While Jesus is never called a mentor in the Bible, He is referred to as rabbi (the Hebrew word for "teacher"). His teachings are still valid for today. They have long outlived the original twelve disciples. In some very real ways, Jesus is still mentoring those who choose to follow Him.

The story of a true miracle is recorded in Acts chapter three when Peter and John, who were both mentored by Jesus, meet a man begging for money as they entered the temple one day. Although neither had any money to offer him, Peter extends a hand to the man and he is miraculously healed! Not long after, Peter and John are accused by the religious leaders of teaching that through Jesus there is a resurrection of the dead (which is true, by the way!) and they were thrown in jail. As confirmation of the power of mentoring they had received from Jesus, we read in Acts 4:13 (emphasis added): *The members of the council were amazed when they saw the boldness of Peter and John, for they could see that they were ordinary men with no special training in the Scriptures.* They also recognized them as men who had been with Jesus. Wow....just wow!

Dr. Chuck Lawless poignantly shares several reasons we all need a mentor by stating:

"(1) It's Biblical. (2) We're created to be in relationship with others. (3) None of us knows everything. (4) All of us have blind spots. (5) Experience is a great teacher. (6) Life will sting sometime. (7) People are God's gift to us." He then goes on to provide some guidelines for finding a mentor. (1) Forget about how old, trained, or smart you are. (2) Pray for a mentor. (3) Look around. (4) Realize that most people have never been a mentor. (5) Ask . . . and keep asking until you find a mentor. (6) Be grateful for whatever a mentor might offer. (7) Invest in somebody else yourself. [2]

- Having a Mentor

Jesus talked about how He was unable to say anything other than what the Father told him to say. Imagine how that impacted His many interactions with the Twelve. These disciples were treated to exclusive, front row seats with the very Son of God as He taught them day by day, year after year. Jesus knew He would not be physically present with the disciples indefinitely. All along, He knew He would return to the Father, send the promised Holy Spirit, and the disciples would take on the work of establishing the church and spreading the Gospel to surrounding nations. Jesus also knew there was no way the Twelve would be up to such a task without pouring His own time and effort into them daily. The coming task was too great. The need to fundamentally alter the direction of mankind was too eternally important to treat lightly. Just as Jesus understood the need for His most trusted disciples to be properly mentored, you, as a secondary leader, need to take that same truth to heart. A recurring theme among this work, nay, even the title itself, is that it is not good for leaders to lead alone. The purposeful interactions between primary and secondary leaders goes to the heart of this work. Primary leaders cannot effectively lead alone; and secondary leaders cannot reach their highest potential without a mentor.

Another classic example of mentoring can be seen as we examine the relationship between the mentor Elijah and the mentee Elisha. We read about this in the book of 1 Kings, but let me begin by providing some background. Elijah was an Old Testament prophet who heard from God and spoke for God: he had received an assignment from God to help guide Israel back into a proper relationship with Him. The first mention of Elijah is found in 1 Kings 17:1 which reads, *Now Elijah, who was from Tishbe in Gilead, told King Ahab, 'As surely as the Lord, the God of Israel, lives - the God I serve - there will be no dew or rain during the next few years until I give the word!'*

Talk about intimidating! Can you imagine God telling you to speak like that to the President of the United States or to the Queen of England? The interesting thing is that speaking boldly against the corruption, idolatry and ungodliness within Israel would be a pattern for Elijah's ministry. The day came, however, when God tells Elijah that he is to find a young man named Elisha and to anoint him as his successor. More specifically, we read in 1 Kings 19:16: ...anoint Elisha son of Shaphat from the town of Abel-meholah to replace you as My prophet.

> The purposeful interactions between primary and secondary leaders goes to the heart of this work. Primary leaders cannot effectively lead alone; and secondary leaders cannot reach their highest potential without a mentor.

For the remaining chapters of 1 Kings and on into 2 Kings, Elijah spends a great amount of time mentoring Elisha for the assignment as his successor. During those days, Elijah would pour into Elisha all he could to make sure he was fully prepared. The culmination of God's calling and Elijah's mentoring is found in 2 Kings 2 where we read how a fiery chariot drawn by horses of fire came from heaven, separating the two men. Elijah was carried to heaven by a whirlwind! Take that, Hollywood theatrics!

Of all that Elisha could have asked from Elijah, his only request is recorded in 2 Kings 2:9 where he says: "Please let me inherit a double share of your spirit and become your successor." The response to Elisha by the prophets from Jericho (2 Kings 2:15) may have been surprising to him, but not to God. He knew Elisha had been mentored and he was ready.

Those who know me well are familiar with how privileged I was to have served alongside Pastor Roger Brumbalow (a.k.a. Bishop) at churches in both New Orleans and Atlanta. He is, and always will be my spiritual father. He took me under his wing for nearly fourteen years. In the truest sense of the word, Bishop mentored me every step of the way by his life, his words and his actions. While I am appreciative of my matriculation and earned degrees, I am even more grateful for being able to attend "Brumbalow University" every day I was privileged to be on his staff. Much like Timothy through Paul, I learned so many things in the moment and through things he experienced long before we began traveling together. Those lessons have stayed with me for all these years – long after his voice was silenced following brain cancer surgery on April

18, 2008. To say that loss created a void in my life – and even more so for his family – would be a gross understatement, indeed. Fortunately, he lived well, he loved well, and he mentored well, so I can still "hear" his voice every single day when making decisions as a leader. Thank you, Bishop, for mentoring me so graciously.

I remember one day, while serving in New Orleans, walking into the church and seeing Bishop standing in a huge trench dug to lay new sewage drainpipes. He spent several years in construction prior to being called into the ministry, so he knew what he was doing. On this day and on many others, he was simply using his gifts to help the church. Mentoring by example helped me in remodeling the church I now serve.

There was another time when he confided in me that he may have to terminate one of the staff members. He asked me to be present when he met with them. I can still recall how awkward and uncomfortable the person appeared to be as he pressed them to either confirm or refute his concerns. The facts he laid out appeared to be undeniable and yet he afforded the person a chance to remain on staff if they were only willing to acknowledge their indiscretion and make the necessary changes. They were not willing, and he had to terminate them. Even in this situation, he did so as gracefully as I think was humanly possible. His example has helped me through the years, especially when I had to fire a staff member.

Then there was the day when he stepped into my office, closed the door and told me, "I've been threatened by one of the men in the church and I'm going to meet him to put an end to this one way or another. This guy is so upset that he will probably bring his gun, and I am not sure what might happen. I need you to drive your car, follow me, park across the street, and be ready to help me if things get out of hand." Thankfully, the meeting went well. Things were resolved in a peaceful way. Here, he served as a mentor by example for the time when I had to meet a guy and put an end to something, one way or another.

Mentorships often are informal. This is fine, but they should always be purposeful. Perhaps you already have a productive relationship with your primary leader, which may cover one or more areas directly related to your core responsibilities. Others from the congregation, your own family, business leaders, and even your hair stylist can serve as mentors in specific areas. Ideally these relationships will be with godly people of strong Christian character, as 1 Corinthians 15:33 reminds us: ...*bad company corrupts good character.*

At the same time, be aware of opportunities to build relationships with others who need to know Christ. You may end up having more influence over them than you could foresee, bearing lasting fruit for the kingdom in the process. Either way, identify relationships with others who have specific insights or skills that you admire, and work to build closer relationships with them. As you do so, think of it along the lines of a long-term payoff. Mentoring certainly is an ongoing process, not an event.

- ## Being a Mentor

Another Biblical example of mentoring is the way Paul mentored his "son in the faith," Timothy. Acts chapter 16 records the initial convergence of their lives: Paul traveled from Derbe to Lystra, where he learned of this young man. It is in verse 2 that we read: *Timothy was well thought of*

> Mentorships often are informal. This is fine, but they should always be purposeful.

by the believers in Lystra and Iconium, so Paul wanted him to join them on their journey. Tradition suggests Paul was forty-eight years old and Timothy was thirty-three years old when this mentoring relationship begins. To that end, Timothy was certainly an adult, but he also needed to be guided by an even more mature adult. Paul was willing to provide the tutelage Timothy needed.

It's uncertain whether or not Timothy began traveling with Paul immediately after being circumcised (verse 3). That is to say, we read that Paul and Silas traveled through the area of Phrygia, Galatia, Troas, and Philippi in Macedonia (verses 6-12) but there is no mention specifically of Timothy. It was while they were in Philippi that Paul and Silas were falsely accused, arrested, imprisoned, and miraculously set free when God sent an earthquake (verses 16-40). Once again, Timothy is not mentioned, but perhaps he was with Paul and Silas. Nonetheless, Timothy would surely be told of these amazing experiences at some point and taught the life-changing principles Paul and Silas discovered. After all, that is precisely what happens in mentoring relationships. Lessons are learned and lessons are shared. Truths are acquired and truths are taught.

The Apostle Paul wrote in 2 Timothy 2:2: *You have heard me teach things that have been confirmed by many reliable witnesses. Now teach these truths to other trustworthy people who will be able to pass them on to others.* Paul penned this very personal letter to Timothy, a textbook mentorship example in its own right. Think of how much time Paul invested in young Timothy and think of the payoff to Paul as well. Paul did not wind-up Timothy and turn him loose, leaving him to his own devices. Timothy stuck around and served very faithfully alongside Paul on multiple missionary journeys, from Corinth to Troas.

Look again at the passage: Paul reflected on the fact he had taught Timothy in many ways, but he did not want it to end there. In the same manner, he wanted Timothy to carry on the tradition of teaching others.

> Lessons are learned and lessons are shared. Truths are acquired and truths are taught.

Paul likely knew at this point that his own days were numbered. Penned from the dark confines of a Roman prison cell and with his execution drawing nearer, this letter to Timothy was one of the last gifts Paul would leave to this world. It is significant that such a parting gift would fall under the domain of mentoring.

Paul brags on Timothy as only a true mentor could do when he says in Philippians 1:19-24 (emphasis added) *If the Lord Jesus is willing,* I hope to send Timothy to you soon *for a visit. Then* he can cheer me up *by telling me how you are getting along.* I have no one else like Timothy, who genuinely cares about your welfare. All the others care only for themselves and not for what matters to Jesus Christ. But you know how Timothy has proved himself. Like a son with his father, he has served with me *in preaching the Good News. I hope to send him to you just as soon as I find out what is going to happen to me here. And I have confidence from the Lord that I myself will come to see you soon."*

Tradition tells us that Timothy died at 80 years of age in AD 97 in the city of Ephesus (where he served as the first Bishop over that city). He was still passionately upholding the truths of the Bible he learned, to a very large degree, from his time with Paul. According to Foxe's Book of Martyrs, "as the pagans were about to celebrate a feast called Catagogion, Timothy, meeting the procession, severely reproved them for their ridiculous idolatry, which so exasperated the people, that they fell upon him with their clubs, and beat him in so dreadful a manner, that he expired of the bruises two days after" (op. cit., p. 20). While the details surrounding the manner and location of his death are uncertain, one thing is clear. Timothy lived by and died for his faith.

Paul understood the value of being a mentor, and so should you. Prayerfully seek out someone who can benefit from your expertise and purposefully work to influence them in ways that advance their personal and spiritual development. Proverbs 27:17 says: *As iron sharpens iron, so a friend sharpens a friend.*

You really have got some sharpening to do...so get busy!

- **Reflect**: Who do you admire that has key traits you are most interested in developing? Who within your current sphere of influence could benefit from your unique skills and experiences?

- **Receive**: Proverbs 9:9: *Instruct the wise, and they will be even wiser. Teach the righteous, and they will learn even more.*

- **Respond**: Remember that mentoring goes both ways – you need one and you need to be one.

MY REFLECTIONS

CHAPTER 16

DO YOU INVEST IN YOUR GROWTH?

No, dear brothers and sisters, I have not achieved it, but I focus on this one thing:
Forgetting the past and looking forward to what lies ahead, I press on
to reach the end of the race and receive the heavenly prize for which God,
through Christ Jesus, is calling us.
(Philippians 3:13-14)

IT was a tale of two workers. A member of our church had two employees, who seemingly could not be more different from each other in terms of the way they approached their jobs. They both showed up faithfully each day and had been employed for several years, but there...the similarities came to an abrupt end.

One constantly looked for ways to make things better; the other did only the bare minimum of what was specifically asked. One worked nights and weekends when needed; the other was usually out the door at five on the dot. They couldn't be bothered to so much as answer a text on the weekend. One communicated constantly; the other had to be endlessly reminded to give basic project status updates. Perhaps their differences were most visible at the time of their annual performance reviews. One could easily show a list of improvements and professional growth during the course of the year, with specific, successful projects to back it up. The other sat there silently, as if a mere spectator, waiting to hear one thing and one thing only – how much of a raise would he get this year?

Year after year, a pattern emerged: the second employee was never happy with his pay. He would go from completely silent to greatly offended when a minimal raise was announced at the end of the review. He wanted to advance within the organization but was unwilling to pay the price to do so. He expected generous opportunities to be handed out, complete with any necessary training (done strictly on company time of course), without impacting his schedule or infringing upon his free time. He seemed unwilling to invest in himself, preferring to blame the company for a stalled career instead of looking inward. Which employee do you think advanced the furthest within that organization? Yep, you are right.

This chapter focuses on personal growth. Specifically, it focuses on the need for leaders to invest in themselves without waiting for anyone else. Are you interested in true, long-term growth? Read on!

There are many points to be made on personal growth. From a Biblical perspective let's begin with a central truth: growth is expected. Christ did not come so we could just barely get by – He came so that we might have life more abundantly. He wants us to grow in many, many ways.

The Apostle Paul had a passion for seeing others grow in their walk with Christ. He was not at all satisfied with the status quo and even berated some of the Corinthian believers for their lack of growth. Writing in 1 Corinthians 3:1-2: *Dear brothers and sisters, when I was with you I couldn't talk to you as I would to spiritual people. I had to talk as though you belonged to this world or as though you were infants in Christ. I had to feed you with milk, not with solid food, because you weren't ready for anything stronger. And you still aren't ready.* Ouch.

> God does not want us to remain where we are, and there is no reason for us to do so. If we look throughout Scripture, we will use words to describe God such as: vibrant, dynamic, vivid, awesome, and radiant.

The writer of Hebrews penned a strikingly similar statement in Hebrews 5:12-14: *You have been believers so long now that* you ought to be teaching others. *Instead, you need someone to teach you again the basic things about God's word.* You are like babies who need milk and cannot eat solid food. *For* someone who lives on milk is still an infant and doesn't know how to do what is right. *Solid food is for those who are mature,* who through training have the skill to recognize the difference between right and wrong (emphasis added).

God does not want us to remain where we are, and there is no reason for us to do so. If we look throughout Scripture, we will use words to describe God such as: vibrant, dynamic, vivid, awesome, and radiant. Just looking out the window at the enormous variety of life He created serves as a perpetual reminder of how He not only created these things, but also makes them grow. As the crowning point of His creation, He certainly wants to see us grow, too!

We looked at some of Paul's words to Timothy in the last chapter which focused on the importance of mentorship. Consider now what Paul writes in 1 Timothy 4:15 when he stresses Timothy's personal responsibility for growth by saying: *Practice these things, immerse yourself in them, so that all may see your progress.* Timothy needed to grow, and Paul saw that clearly.

> Let's make this personal: whether you would receive five talents, two talents, or one talent, your job is to take what you have been entrusted with and run with it.

If our first reaction to growth is excitement, then our second reaction is usually fear. Growth carries risks. Let's address that impediment to growth head-on. I would like to tell you that you shouldn't be afraid of growth. I would also like to tell you I've never been afraid of it myself. The reality is that fear is sometimes a legitimate human emotion and, along with a heathy dose of godly wisdom and the Holy Spirit's urging, can be a great deterrent to hastily embarking upon a foolish endeavor. Nonetheless, we need to prayerfully move beyond this fear when we know God is leading us in a given direction.

Let me begin by confessing I did not complete my undergraduate degree until I was forty years old. Upon graduating from high school, I had been offered a partial basketball scholarship to a junior college in Texas. I declined for several reasons – mainly so I could stay close to Missy, as our relationship was growing. In addition, I had been offered a full academic scholarship to Northeast Louisiana University (now the University of Louisiana at Monroe) which I accepted. My goal was to obtain a mechanical engineering degree and make lots of money! Unfortunately, I lost that full scholarship in my first semester due to my failing grades caused by spending way too much time playing pool and drinking way too much alcohol. Those were certainly not some of my proudest moments.

My life eventually began to change on February 7, 1982 which is when I truly began a personal relationship with Jesus Christ. I started working for the Ouachita Coca-Cola Bottling Company and quickly moved through the ranks from sales into management. It was during that time my Dad bought a business, Missy and I married, and we entered the ministry on the same weekend we came home from our honeymoon. Our first son would be born not quite two years later, we would move to New Orleans where our daughter would be born. We then moved to Atlanta five years later. It seemed my dream of finishing college might never happen.

After being in Atlanta for five years, I was given an opportunity to resume my academic pursuits. I did so when I was thirty-seven years of age. In telling our children that I was going back to college, I can still remember Summer asking, "Daddy, how long will it take you to graduate?" I told her it would take about three years. She followed up by asking, "Daddy, how old will you be when you graduate?" I told her, "I will be forty years old when I graduate." Summer looked surprised! I followed up by asking, "But how old will I be in three years even if I don't go back to school?" I went on to receive an undergraduate degree from Beulah Heights University and humbly accepted my diploma from Dr. Samuel Chand at forty years of age. I would go on to obtain a Master of Arts degree and my plans are to pursue a doctorate in the near future. Regardless of your age or stage in life, you must invest in yourself in order to grow.

The Parable of the Talents found in Matthew chapter 25 comes to mind here. You'll remember the guy who had been given only one bag of silver, or one talent. When the master returned and asked him for an account, he replied, "I was afraid I would lose your money, so I hid it in the earth." In fairness to each of the three servants to whom the master had entrusted his wealth, no instructions were given. No hot stock tips were provided and no financial reports on upcoming global trade trends were offered to give clues on how the money should be invested for an optimal return. The master simply divided his wealth among them and took off on a long journey.

Yet the master clearly expected them to take what they had been given and – according to their ability – use it and make it grow. Let's make this personal: whether you would receive five talents, two talents, or one talent, your job is to take what you have been entrusted with and run with it.

- If the talent has already been buried in your backyard, grab a shovel and dig it back up.

- If God has placed a particular area of ministry on your heart and nothing has happened yet, make something happen, however small it might seem. Prepare yourself; read a book on it; talk to someone who is already involved; ask for a small assignment in that area. Prove yourself faithful in a small thing, and you're more likely to receive a larger opportunity.

- Expect nothing to be easy and accept any failures along the way as part of the price of your eventual success. Very few men and women succeed wildly upon their first attempt; most work past obstacles and initial failures on their way to something greater.

- Speaking of failures, think back on previous failures where you simply gave up. Was it truly a failure? Was it instead a lesson on how not to do something? There was an important reason you made the first attempt. Pick it back up and try again.

I believe our Master in heaven has a very different view of success and failure than we do. If it feels like the world wants to see you fail, you're probably right. Legendary football coach Lou Holtz even quipped,

> "Never tell your problems to anyone…20% don't care and the other 80% are glad you have them."[1]

There are plenty of naysayers out there hoping you'll slip up and fall so they can say they told you so. In many of these cases, those who want to see you fail are the same ones who are unable to push past their own fears and strive for something truly great. Why should they be the standard to which we compare ourselves?

Christ, on the other hand, wants you to thrive and be victorious in whatever capacity He has designated for you. Therefore, the concept of true defeat needs to be eliminated from our vocabularies. Instead, we need to focus on the truth of Romans 8:37 which says that come what may: *overwhelming victory is ours through Christ.* Rest in that and go for it.

There are, however, some myths surrounding growth. At first glance, the word connotes vibrancy, excitement, and promise. We marvel at churches experiencing rapid growth, or we admire companies doing so well they cannot handle all the business that people send their way. Every online seller

> There are plenty of naysayers out there hoping you'll slip up and fall so they can say they told you so. In many of these cases, those who want to see you fail are the same ones who are unable to push past their own fears and strive for something truly great.

wants to overtake Amazon and exceed their sales many times over. The truth is that while growth spurts can be wildly exhilarating, growth typically is a very slow process. Growth is usually boring.

What I mean by that is that when an athlete wants to grow, he doesn't do so on the world stage. It happens in a gym, alone on night after dreary night, lifting ever slightly more weight today than he did yesterday. Next week, he'll lift slightly more weight again. Gains in terms of the amount lifted per repetition may be measured in as few as five pounds over the course of a month. That is hardly exciting! "Hey guys, I just bench pressed three sets of five with one hundred seventy-five pounds instead of last month's three sets of five with one hundred seventy pounds!" Not too many people will applaud such a modest gain, will they?

Muhammad Ali once quipped:

"I hated every minute of training, but I said, 'Don't quit. Suffer now and live the rest of your life as a champion.'"[2]

Despite the claims he made about himself, Muhammad Ali is arguably the greatest heavyweight boxing champion of all time. He paid the price. He trained. He won one fight at a time.

That is the nature of growth – small, consistent steps taken over a long period of time that take the athlete to a whole new level. The same is often true in our spiritual growth. Things usually do not happen overnight. As the Parable of the Talents illustrates, success is measured in terms of faithfulness, steadiness, and consistency to take whatever we have been given and make it grow. It has little to do with how quickly we reach a certain point.

The growth pattern of the Chinese bamboo tree is remarkable. Plant a bamboo sprout in the ground and for four or five years (sometimes much longer), nothing happens. You must water and fertilize it frequently but there is no visible evidence that anything is happening. Nothing. Nada. Zilch. About the fifth year, things change quickly and quite dramatically. In only a six-week period, the Chinese bamboo tree grows to a staggering ninety feet tall. That's right, ninety feet tall! Some people mistakenly think it experiences astronomical growth in six weeks, but you already know that it really grows in about five years. If you were to stop providing routine, mundane, boring care at any time then the growth would never take place.

In Philippians 3:13-14, Paul acknowledges that he hasn't yet arrived, but he continues to press on toward the prize. In terms of your personal growth, what are you pressing toward?

- **Reflect:** Take a few minutes to make a list of ten areas in which you would like to see personal or professional growth. Then order them by their relative importance to you.

- **Receive:** 2 Peter 3:18: *Rather, you must grow in the grace and knowledge of our Lord and Savior Jesus Christ. All glory to Him, both now and forever! Amen.*

- **Respond:** From the list above, what steps do you need to take to instigate growth in the areas most important to you? Remember that growth starts with small steps. What small steps can you take this week to bring you closer to where you want to be?

MY REFLECTIONS

CHAPTER 17

ARE YOU PREPARING FOR YOUR FUTURE?

*Take a lesson from the ants, you lazybones. Learn from their ways
and become wise! Though they have no prince or governor or ruler
to make them work, they labor hard all summer, gathering food for the winter.
But you, lazybones, how long will you sleep? When will you wake up?
A little extra sleep, a little more slumber, a little folding of the hands to rest –
then poverty will pounce on you like a bandit; scarcity will attack you
like an armed robber.*
(Proverbs 6:6-11)

REGARDLESS of the position in which you currently serve, I'm guessing you would really like to climb the corporate ladder or move up in your organization. That is to say, you have dreams and aspirations of doing more and going higher. I suspect most primary leaders would rather have employees who are more like racehorses (who must be reined in at times) than like lazy mules (who have to be dragged out of the barn)!

Having said that, I do know a wonderful secondary leader who will passionately admit he knows where he best fits in his organization. He is content to serve in that capacity for the rest of his working years. Because I know him personally, I can attest to the fact he has a great heart and he is a true servant, who is of tremendous value to his primary leader.

Which is right? Drive and ambition or consistency and contentment? I say both can be right, but both still come with an expectation and need for the person to prepare for the future. Whether you remain in your current position forever or you transition several more times, tomorrow is a day for which you must be prepared.

Burt Nanus helps us to understand the dynamic tension that constantly exists within the a leader who is simultaneously trying to focus on today and on tomorrow.

"The ability to think about the future is a distinctly human quality that sets us apart from all other species. This ability enables us to act not just in response to an actual physical stimulus, as all other animals do, but also to images of future worlds that exist only in the mind."[1]

Therein lies the struggle every leader faces on a daily basis.

Some people tragically misinterpret the words of Jesus in Matthew 6:34 as if He were saying we do not need to be prepared. Nothing could be further from the truth. What He actually said is, *Don't worry about tomorrow, for tomorrow will bring its own worries. Today's trouble is enough for today.* What He did not say is "Don't be prepared for tomorrow, for you have already prepared enough. Today's preparation is enough to last you for the rest of your life." In the context of Matthew chapter 6, Jesus emphasized His followers do not have to worry about tomorrow, because God knows what they need. He will faithfully provide.

The word "prepare" literally means "to make ready beforehand for some purpose, use, or activity." As time continues, you will always need to prepare for the future. In fact, Solomon tells us in Proverbs 6:8 that ants work hard all summer, gathering the food they will eat in the winter. Since ants are smart enough to prepare for their future, we should be prepared, too. Proverbs 22:3 says: *A prudent person foresees danger and takes precautions. The simpleton goes blindly on and suffers the consequences.* Notice the contrast Solomon creates by describing two very different people. Being a prudent person means you give careful thought about the future. Being a simpleton means you are careless and lack common sense.

> Which is right? Drive and ambition or consistency and contentment? I say both can be right, but both still come with an expectation and need for the person to prepare for the future.

Consider the story of Joseph and you will see how it speaks to the need for preparation. Genesis 37:1-2 says: *Jacob settled again in the land of Canaan, where his father had lived as a foreigner. This is the account of Jacob and his family. When Joseph was seventeen years old, he often tended his father's flocks.* Like most of the youngest sons in these times, Joseph is responsible for being the family shepherd. It was not a prominent position at all. Shepherds were often despised and rejected by society, even though their role was very important in this period. Without shepherds, there would be no sheep.

We also discover something else about Joseph from Genesis 37:3: *Jacob loved Joseph more than any of his other children because Joseph had been born to him in his old age. So one day Jacob had a special gift made for Joseph - a beautiful robe.* Joseph was Jacob's favorite son. Everyone knew it because of the way Jacob treated him. They were reminded Joseph was the favorite by the decorative robe he wore. Like any sibling who felt overlooked and underappreciated, it is no surprise to read in Genesis 37:4: *But his brothers hated Joseph because their father loved him more than the rest of them. They couldn't say a kind word to him.*

God eventually gave Joseph two unique dreams pointing to his destiny (which would be fulfilled in the future). As a result, Joseph's brothers hated him even more. It finally reached the boiling point when they conspired to kill him. Thankfully, Reuben intervened, explaining to the others that their father would mourn himself to death if Joseph were to die. After some discussion, they decided to throw him in a pit where he would eventually die on his own. Then the brothers saw a caravan of traders passing by and they decided to sell Joseph to them to get rid of him. Joseph ended up in Egypt, where he became Potiphar's slave (the captain of the palace guard working for Pharaoh). None of this seems to be pointing to Joseph's divinely inspired future.

But wait for it.

After serving in their home for some time, Potiphar notices the Lord is with Joseph, giving him success in everything that he does. Potiphar places Joseph in charge of all his personal business. As a result, God blesses Potiphar because of Joseph's presence. Potiphar could not have been more pleased. Joseph's destiny seems to be coming to fruition as he prospers in Egypt, despite being a slave. On many levels, it looks like things are finally turning around for him and perhaps his dreams are coming true – just not how he originally thought.

In Genesis chapter 39 we read that Potiphar's wife was attracted to Joseph. She began trying to seduce him into having an affair. Because of Joseph's unwavering devotion to God, he refuses her advances, but she continues pursuing him on a daily basis. Joseph tells her, *Look, my master trusts me with everything in his entire household. No one here has more authority than I do. He has held back nothing from me except you, because you are his wife. How could I do such a wicked thing? It would be a great sin against God.* It is apparent from his response that Joseph knew having an affair with Potiphar's wife was not what was needed to prepare for his future.

Despite being resolute in his commitment to God and to doing the right thing, Potiphar's wife was relentless in trying to seduce Joseph. Genesis 39:10-12 says: *She kept putting pressure on Joseph day after day, but he refused to sleep with her, and he kept out of her way as much as possible. One day, however, no one else was around when he went in to do his work. She came and grabbed him by his cloak, demanding, 'Come on, sleep with me! Joseph tore himself away, but he left his cloak in her hand as he ran from the house.* In a desperate attempt to get away, Joseph took off running with Potiphar's wife clinging to his cloak. What happened next reveals just how evil this woman was and the lengths to which she would go to ruin Joseph's life.

In summary: she screams, the servants come running into the room, she tells them Joseph tried to rape her, and she repeats the same lies to Potiphar when he gets home. As most husbands would do, Potiphar believes his wife and has Joseph thrown into prison where he remained for quite some time. It is then we read in Genesis 39:20-23: *But the Lord was with Joseph in the prison and showed him His faithful love. And the Lord made Joseph a favorite with the prison warden. Before long, the warden put Joseph in charge of all the other prisoners and over everything that happened in the prison. The warden had no more worries, because Joseph took care of everything. The Lord was with him and caused everything he did to succeed.*

While remaining in prison, Joseph accurately interprets the dreams of Pharaoh's chief cupbearer and chief baker and their lives end up just as Joseph said. Two years later, Pharaoh has a dream that his wise men and magicians cannot interpret. At this time, the chief cupbearer remembers Joseph. He tells Pharaoh Joseph can interpret his dream, so Pharoah calls for Joseph to be brought to him.

Joseph tells Pharaoh the meaning of his dreams and Pharaoh is so impressed he says, *Can we find anyone else like this man so obviously filled with the spirit of God?* We now see the result of Joseph's preparation throughout his life in Genesis 41:39-44: *Then Pharaoh said to Joseph, 'Since God has revealed the meaning of the dreams to you, clearly no one else is as intelligent or wise as you are. You will be in charge of my court, and all my people will take orders from you. Only I, sitting on my throne, will have a rank higher than yours.' Pharaoh said to Joseph, 'I hereby put you in charge of the entire land of Egypt.' Then Pharaoh removed his signet ring from his hand and placed it on Joseph's finger. He dressed him in fine linen clothing and hung a gold chain around his neck. Then he had Joseph ride in the chariot reserved for his second-in-command. And wherever Joseph went, the command was shouted,*

'Kneel down!' So Pharaoh put Joseph in charge of all Egypt. And Pharaoh said to him, 'I am Pharaoh, but no one will lift a hand or foot in the entire land of Egypt without your approval.'

Wait a minute! Did we correctly read Joseph, who is hated by his brothers...and is a Hebrew slave who was falsely accused of raping his master's wife...and who has been sitting in an Egyptian prison for years, has just been promoted to being second in command, with only Pharaoh more powerful than he? Through all of the negative things he experienced and all of the various roles he filled, Joseph had been prepared for this promotion. He was ready for whatever would lie before him!

> God decides today what He can trust you with tomorrow. Be faithful today, or He will never trust you with more tomorrow.

And, you may ask, What about his brothers? Well, the day would come when a famine would devastate the food supply in their country, so they travelled to Egypt to buy food. They had no idea what had happened to Joseph after they sold him into slavery. They end up standing before Joseph, but they didn't recognize him. It wasn't until he revealed his identity that they realized who he was. Then, they were terrified, expecting him to have them killed.

Genesis 45:4-8 gives us a glimpse into the heart of Joseph towards his brothers: *'Please, come closer,' he said to them. So they came closer. And he said again, 'I am Joseph, your brother, whom you sold into slavery in Egypt. But don't be upset, and don't be angry with yourselves for selling me to this place. It was God Who sent me here ahead of you to preserve your lives. This famine that has ravaged the land for two years will last five more years, and there will be neither plowing nor harvesting. God has sent me ahead of you to keep you and your families alive and to preserve many survivors. So it was God Who sent me here, not you! And He is the One Who made me an adviser to Pharaoh - the manager of his entire palace and the governor of all Egypt.'* Even though he could have snapped his fingers or waved his hand and had them killed, Joseph interprets the events of his life through the lens of divine purpose. He realizes God has prepared him for this moment in order to fulfill the purposes for which God had created him.

The life of David also reinforces the importance of being prepared for the future. 1 Samuel 16:1-3 records: *Now the Lord said to Samuel, 'You have mourned long enough for Saul. I have rejected him as king of Israel, so fill your flask with olive oil and go to Bethlehem. Find a man named*

esse who lives there, for I have selected one of his sons to be my king.'
But Samuel asked, 'How can I do that? If Saul hears about it, he will kill
me.' 'Take a heifer with you,' the Lord replied, 'and say that you have
come to make a sacrifice to the Lord. Invite Jesse to the sacrifice, and I
will show you which of his sons to anoint for Me.' On the surface, these
verses do not tell us anything about David, but read on.

Samuel goes to the house of Jesse, fully prepared to anoint the next
king of Israel. As would have been the case in their culture, Jesse sends
in his first son, Eliab. The Lord tells Samuel he is not the one. Jesse ends
up sending six more of his sons, but Samuel tells Jesse the Lord has not
chosen any of them. What Samuel does next opens the door for David,
when he asks Jesse if he has any more sons. Jesse replies: *There is still*
the youngest. But he's out in the fields watching the sheep and goats.
Wow...talk about a father who seemingly had no confidence in his boy!
After watching his biggest and best sons be passed up as Israel's next
king, it is doubtful Jesse could fathom that David had any chance either.

I Samuel 16:11-13 says: *'Send for him at once,' Samuel said. 'We will*
not sit down to eat until he arrives.' So Jesse sent for him. He was dark
and handsome, with beautiful eyes. And the Lord said, 'This is the one;
anoint him.' So as David stood there among his brothers, Samuel took
the flask of olive oil he had brought and anointed David with the oil. And
the Spirit of the Lord came powerfully upon David from that day on. Then
Samuel returned to Ramah. David may not have been chosen by his
dad or his brothers, but God chose him! They may have lacked
confidence in David, seeing him as no more than a shepherd...but God
knew he could be king one day.

Those verses are among the most encouraging portions of scripture
for every underdog who nobody thinks can beat the champion, for every
kid who is always picked last on the playground, and for every adult who
thinks they are stuck in their current position with no hope for doing
anything greater! Don't ever let anybody tell you that you can't do what
God has called you to do. With His help and with your preparation, you
can do anything!

As you may know, David did not leave the anointing service, go to
his room, pack his clothes and move right into the palace to begin his
reign as King of Israel. Nothing could be further from the truth. Although
his precise age is not provided, on the day he was anointed, we can
presume he was less than fifteen years old.

In the days to follow, Jesse will send David to deliver bread and
cheese to his brothers. David now becomes a delivery boy. While on that
assignment, David learns how the Philistine giant Goliath is threatening

the army of Israel. Here, he volunteers to fight him. David now becomes a giant killer. When the people celebrate David's victory, King Saul becomes jealous. He tries to kill David on more than one occasion. David is then a fugitive, running for his life.

This process takes years. All the while, David is prepared for his future. 2 Samuel 5:4 tell us: *David was thirty years old when he began to reign, and he reigned forty years in all.* David is anointed as a young boy, but it took at least fifteen years before he sat upon the throne in Israel. Some would say those were wasted years. God would say those were preparation years.

Think about this for a moment: The disciples were more than just associates to Jesus. They were more than just secondary leaders. They were primary leaders in training for things they would do in the future. Sure, they had important roles to fill as they followed Jesus, but He knew that would not be all they did. In other words, they had to prepare for the future. The future would surely come sooner than they imagined. After only about three years of walking with Jesus, the disciples would be faced with His death, burial, resurrection, and ascension. Jesus promised the Holy Spirit would be with them and in them, because He knew they would be afraid of being alone.

What did the disciples do after Jesus ascended to heaven? Peter preached on the Day of Pentecost and three thousand people were saved and baptized. Not bad for his first sermon! All the disciples were greatly used by God to take the Gospel to the entire known world, preaching and teaching, building churches and raising up leaders. If they had failed in their mission, the church might not have survived past the first generation of Christ followers. Thankfully they did not fail, and the Church has continued for over two thousand years!

God decides today what He can trust you with tomorrow. Be faithful today, or He will never trust you with more tomorrow.

- **Reflect:** Think back on the most painful experiences of your life. Can you see how God was there and how He has actually been preparing you for your purpose?

- **Receive:** Romans 8:28: *We know that God causes everything to work together for the good of those who love God and are called according to his purpose for them.*

- **Respond:** In light of what you have learned in this chapter, how can you better prepare for your future?

MY REFLECTIONS

CHAPTER 18

CAN YOU FOLLOW DIRECTIONS?

The Lord says, "I will guide you along the best pathway for your life.
I will advise you and watch over you."
(Psalm 32:8)

HAVE you ever heard the saying, "When all else fails, read the directions?" As a father, I can still remember staying up half the night on Christmas Eve, scrambling to put together a gift for our young children. I know full well that Christmas Day is December 25 every year, so it wasn't like I was caught off guard or I had forgotten the gifts needed to be put together. It's just we had no place to hide something, unless they stayed in the small boxes leading up to Christmas.

I need to confess something before I go much further. None of the Osbon men are known to have the patience of Job; I might win the award for being the least patient at times. The title is not a noble one, but one that I must admit I have earned on some occasions.

Back to the assembling of Christmas gifts on Christmas Eve. More times than I care to admit, I have found myself getting to the end of what I thought was the process only to discover – much to my chagrin – that I either have extra parts left over or I don't have enough parts. It's now 2:38 AM, the stores are all closed, the kids will be up in a couple of hours, I need to get a little sleep, and we have a problem! Of course, if I had only read and followed the directions, I probably would have gotten to sleep much earlier, with no missing or extra parts.

When all else fails, read the directions. This applies to swing sets, bicycles, IKEA furniture and whatever your boss asks you to do. For the rest of your career, the chances are great you will always have someone to report to or someone who is over you. This will be the case regardless of whether you work in corporate America or in the church. Even the CEO and the Pastor are accountable to and answerable to someone other than themselves.

Whenever a leader creates an assignment, the leader expects the staff member knows what to do, has the experience to accomplish the task, possesses the skills necessary to accomplish the task, and whatever other resources might be needed. The leader expects the staff member to do whatever it takes to ensure the assignment is fulfilled. If there are any obstacles which cannot be overcome or the task cannot be completed in a timely manner, the leader expects such to be reported to them. Beyond these things, the leader expects to receive a final report from the staff member, acknowledging the assignment has been completed up to and beyond the leader's expectations.

Sounds easy enough, right? Not necessarily.

Can I share one more confession with you? Nearly every leader I know would say they spend a great deal more time than they should following up with their staff to see if assignments are being completed. In fact, some would say doing so is one of their greatest frustrations and time thieves. What does that mean? Let me explain.

Every leader with multiple staff members works with very different individuals. Each has their own unique gifts and personality. Each one possesses different ways to approach and process an assignment. While that is a given, what is often not understood by the staff is that the leader is responsible for the organization and must ensure it operates at the highest level of excellence. Every time a leader must ask a staff member about an assignment is time the leader cannot spend on his or her primary responsibilities. Admittedly, the leader's job is to oversee the entire organization; however, the staff members could help him do his job better if they would just follow the directions they have already received.

In Exodus chapters 25-30, God gives Moses very detailed directions on how He wants the Ark of the Covenant, the table of shewbread, the lampstand, the Tabernacle, the altar, the courtyard, the priest's clothing, the ephod, the chest piece, the incense altar, the washbasin, the anointing oil, the incense and many other items to be used in Israel's worship to the Lord. In addition, God gives Moses very detailed directions on how to dedicate the priests, what they are to wear, and the specifics of this very elaborate ceremony.

In Exodus chapter 31 God tells Moses that He has given special gifts to various artisans, to whom he is to assign the responsibility of building and creating all these things. In other words, God knew Moses could not do it alone and it would take an entire team (a.k.a. staff) to accomplish the work. God is into the details! He makes certain to communicate them clearly to Moses, but He also expects Moses to lead the team to ensure it is all done correctly. In fact, God says in Exodus 31:11b, *The craftsmen must make everything* as I have commanded you. (emphasis added).

You can read about the building of the tabernacle and the other items in Exodus chapters 36-39. As you will see, God clearly told Moses what He wanted, Moses made the assignments clear, and the people followed the directions given by Moses. We know that to be the case because Exodus 39:42-43 says: *So the people of Israel followed all of the Lord's instructions to Moses. Then Moses inspected all their work. When he found it had been done just as the Lord had commanded him, he blessed them.* In addition, Exodus 40:16 says: *Moses proceeded to do everything just as the Lord had commanded him.* In other words, Moses knew how to follow the directions. Mission accomplished!

> Every leader with multiple staff members works with very different individuals. Each has their own unique gifts and personality. Each one possesses different ways to approach and process an assignment.

You can read about directions God later gave to Moses and Aaron in Numbers chapter two. In this portion, God lays out the specific places each of the tribes of Israel were to camp around the Tabernacle. The tribes of Judah, Issachar and Zebulun were to pitch their tents on the east side; Reuben, Simeon and Gad on the south side; Ephraim, Manasseh and Benjamin camped on the west side; and Dan, Asher and Naphtali set up on the north side of the Tabernacle. We may never fully understand the rationale behind the placement of the tribes, and we may tend to think it really doesn't matter. God, however, knows the exact reasons, which is why He gave such specific directions. He did not leave it up to Moses or Aaron, because God always knows best.

Every. Single. Time.

Let me ask you a couple of questions. Would your leader say you are the type of staff member who receives an assignment, follows directions and does not need constant reminders to ensure you stay on task? If so, then I can tell you are the type of team member every leader would absolutely love to have on their staff. They would probably love to clone you! In contrast, would your leader say you are the type of staff member who receives an assignment, but then he must regularly follow up with you to make sure the assignments are completed in a timely manner and according to the directions? If so then, very simply put, I can tell your leader desperately needs you to improve in this area. The sooner, the better.

According to an article written by Becky Vaughn-Furlow, here are fifteen tips on how to be a better follower once you have been given directions from your leader:[1]

- Listen carefully. Pay attention.

- Ask questions if there is a lack of understanding.

- Follow the leader's instructions.

- If for some reason, you cannot do what is asked, speak up.

- Have a positive attitude.

- Take care of your part of the work and don't be concerned about others' roles.

- If you complete your work, offer to help someone else.

- Don't be concerned if the specific task is not spelled out in your job description.

- If asked about something for which you don't have an answer, get an answer.

- Go to your supervisor to find the answer, not to others who don't know or to social media.

- When you have the answer, be sure you relay it to the person who inquired.

- Don't complain or whine.

- Take notes.

- Make a checklist.

- Go the extra mile and provide good customer service.

Does that sound too basic, almost like you are back in kindergarten? While I wish it were not true, it seems too many people simply do not have a thorough grasp of what it takes to follow directions.

While serving at a previous church, one of my responsibilities was to ensure care of the facilities and supervision of the custodial staff. For several years, a precious older man worked for me, who we affectionately called Brother John. He loved his Lord, and he loved his job! During the hiring process, I gave Brother John very clear guidelines on what would be expected of him, along with a daily schedule of areas which would need cleaning. All of this was coordinated based on the typical worship schedule, but it was adjusted for special activities and services. Brother John always arrived to work early. I never had to worry about finding him slacking off in any way. He was faithful and diligent.

Over the course of time, I noticed a pattern with Brother John anytime I would stop his work and ask him to do something else that needed attention. Many times, I would tell him it was fine to complete this new task later on, but I wanted to mention it to him before I forgot. Almost without exception, Brother John would turn off the vacuum cleaner or set down the mop and head off to the part of the building where the new assignment was located.

At first, I reminded him that he did not need to stop what he was doing. Later, I stopped reminding him after he gave me the same response a couple of times. He would say, "I know that I won't forget what I'm doing right now, but I am going to take care of that to make sure that I don't forget." He would then quickly head over to the new assignment, complete it, and return to what he had been doing when I interrupted him. Both assignments were completed with excellence. During all the years Brother John worked for me, I don't ever recall a single time that I had to ask him if he had completed an assignment. Brother John served with excellence, he served with diligence, and he never forgot a thing. I never even saw him write

Would your leader say you are the type of staff member who receives an assignment, but then he must regularly follow up with you to make sure the assignments are completed in a timely manner and according to the directions? If so then, very simply put, I can tell your leader desperately needs you to improve in this area.

anything down. He was amazing, absolutely amazing!

Now, the truth is, everyone is not a twin of Brother John. Most people need to write things down, make calendar notes and schedule cell phone reminders, or else they will forget a lot of important things. Confession time. I am one of those people. You might be blown away if you were take a look at my Outlook calendar, which is full of entries that I make to (hopefully) help me not to forget appointments, commitments and important events. Here is just one example of what works for me: Let's say I have a Zoom meeting at 2:00PM on Thursday. I calendar the appointment on Thursday at 2:00pm, I calendar a reminder at 1:30PM to set up for the Zoom meeting, I calendar a "Don't forget the 2:00PM Zoom meeting" reminder at 8:00AM and 10:00AM that day and at 9:00PM on the night before! Additionally, when I give a staff member an assignment, I oftentimes give them a deadline and immediately create a calendar called "Due Date." This they receive via Outlook, to add to their calendar. I can almost hear you laughing at me as you are reading this, but that's OK! I have a system that works for me, and I do not forget important things because I use my system.

Stop laughing for a minute and consider these questions. Do you have a system? Is it working, or are you still forgetting things? If you don't have a system, your leader needs you to create one and the sooner, the better. He or she should not even have to ask you about an assignment once it has been made. I will even go so far as to say it is a waste of their time to follow up to see if you're doing your job. Be a Brother John and do whatever it takes to be a faithful, diligent staff member.

- **Reflect:** Think back on a time when you had difficulty completing a task and you now realize it was because you did not follow the directions. How did you feel then? How do you feel now?

- **Receive:** Proverbs 1:8: *...listen when your father corrects you. Don't neglect your mother's instruction.*

- **Respond:** Decide today to closely follow the directions you receive so the tasks you are given can be successfully completed.

MY REFLECTIONS

CHAPTER 19

WHAT IF YOUR LEADER IS A LOSER?

Potiphar was furious when he heard his wife's story about how Joseph had treated her. So he took Joseph and threw him into the prison where the king's prisoners were held, and there he remained.
(Genesis 39:19-20, NLT)

THIS may be the most controversial subject within this book. No one wants to think it could possibly be God's plan for them to work for someone who did not have their best interest at heart or who might treat them in ways far less than they deserve. At some point in our lives, we may end up working for and serving someone who fits that description. Because this may happen, it is important to know what we should do. In my estimation, there is no better place to look than within the pages of God's Word which, fortunately for us, contains the good, the bad and the ugly stories of those who have gone before us.

Even a cursory review of the Bible will lead us to acknowledge some of God's choicest servants were subjected to the reality that they were being asked – in some cases, even required - to serve leaders who were not worthy of their service. Names such as Joseph, David and Daniel come to mind. The list, however, goes on and on. The experience does not stop with the last chapter of the Bible; this truth exists in modernity, as well. Even to this day, men and women who strive to faithfully live out their faith on their jobs are confronted with the sobering reality that their leader does not share their same morals and values. When that occurs – and it does quite frequently – the questions loom. What am I to do? What does God expect? Should I quit and find another leader who is more like me?

We read in Genesis chapter 37 that Joseph was the favorite son of his father, Jacob. This may have afforded Joseph a beautiful coat of many colors, but it also attracted the envy and jealousy of Joseph's brothers. Over the course of time, his brothers began to hate Joseph more and more. It reached the point where they decided they would throw him into a well and tell Jacob he had been killed by a wild animal. As their conversation continued, a caravan of Midianite traders passed by, and the brothers sold Joseph to them as a slave. They thought this would get rid of Joseph and provide them with some money in return. When they arrived in Egypt, the traders sold Joseph to Potiphar, one of Pharaoh's officers, to be his personal slave.

As you may recall, Joseph was an Israelite with a distinct heritage of being from a line of godly ancestors. Albeit none of them were perfect, some of the prominent patriarchs of the Jewish faith are Joseph's family members such as his great-grandfather Abraham and his father Jacob. Joseph grew up in and wholeheartedly embraced his Jewish faith which was the guiding force for his values, his morals, and his entire life. To that end, it is reasonable to presume Joseph experienced culture shock upon arriving in Egypt and as he witnessed the idolatry and paganism commonplace in this new land where he now lived. To say that Joseph's faith was challenged would be an understatement.

Genesis 39:2 says (emphasis added): *The Lord was with Joseph, so he succeeded in everything he did* as he served in the home of his Egyptian master. Wait, what? Did you catch those truths? God was with Joseph in this pagan land! He caused Joseph to succeed in everything he did as he served his ungodly master, Potiphar! Could it be possible that the same things are true with you, my friend? I believe so! I pray you will discover them on a daily basis, as you serve even under the most difficult of circumstances.

> Even a cursory review of the Bible will lead us to acknowledge some of God's choicest servants were subjected to the reality that they were being asked – in some cases, even required – to serve leaders who were not worthy of their service.

David is twice referred to by God as *a man after My own heart* (1 Samuel 13:14, Acts 13:22). It would certainly seem apparent that David was a very godly man who tried to live for God. Once again, David was not perfect, but he did receive God's accolade. This means he must have been a faithful man, nonetheless. It is wise for me to insert at this point that no one who has ever lived – except Jesus – was perfect. At that end, perhaps we should not be too quick to look down on others who are just like us – imperfect in many ways.

1 Samuel chapter 16 records for us the first mention of David in

the Bible as Samuel is sent by God to the house of Jesse to anoint one of his sons to be the next king of Israel. After seven of Jesse's sons come into the room and all seven are not God's choice, Samuel asks if Jesse has any more sons and he replies in verse 11: *There is still the youngest. But he's out in the fields watching the sheep and goats.* Samuel's response still causes me to pause as he says, *Send for him at once. We will not sit down to eat until he arrives.* I hope the magnitude of those words resonates in your spirit like they do in mine! There are some assignments God has for you that will cause people to stay standing until you show up. Only you can fulfill what God is asking you to do — and they know it!

We then read in 1 Samuel 16:12b-13b: *And the Lord said, 'This is the one; anoint him.' So as David stood there among his brothers, Samuel took the flask of olive oil he had brought and anointed David with the oil. And the Spirit of the Lord came powerfully upon David from that day on.* Here I'll add some clarification to avoid any potential confusion. Unlike what we may tend to believe, David did not immediately ascend to the throne as King of Israel. Nothing could be further from the truth! What happened here is a story every leader should read.

Although there is some ambiguity as to his exact age, many scholars presume David was around fifteen years old when he was anointed by Samuel. We do know with certainty he was still less than twenty years old when he visits his brothers on the battlefield (at which time he kills Goliath), as all males of that age were required to be in the military. Over the course of the next several years, David would live and survive under the ungodly leadership of King Saul. It was during those years David would dodge spears as Saul tried to kill him and live in caves as Saul tried to hunt him down. Although he had the chance to take Saul's life, David continued to perceive him as "the Lord's anointed." He refused to get revenge to assume his rightful place upon the throne. Those were some of David's darkest years, but God was faithful, and He kept His promise.

2 Samuel 5:4-5 tell us David was thirty years old when he became King and he reigned over Israel for forty years. I suspect David applied many leadership lessons he learned through faithfully serving Saul as he ruled over God's people. Truth be told, some of us have learned how "not" to lead during our time of serving others as well as how "to" lead. Both are equally important and can only be learned through both positive and negative experiences.

> There are some assignments God has for you that will cause people to stay standing until you show up. Only you can fulfill what God is asking you to do – and they know it!

Much like Joseph and David, a young man named Daniel provides us with similar leadership lessons. From these, we can learn from the far-less-than-perfect leaders we serve. Daniel chapter 1 records how God allowed King Nebuchadnezzar (from Babylon) to defeat King Jehoiakim of Judah. In doing so, Nebuchadnezzar took captive many young men from Judah's royal family and began to indoctrinate them into Babylonian language and literature.

Despite his inability to change his circumstances or his surroundings, Daniel remained committed to his Jewish faith and to his God. He refused to defile himself in any way. Over the years to come, Daniel would be promoted and imprisoned, but God's favor remained upon his life.

Daniel would be gifted by God with the ability to interpret dreams. This ability would be used to position Daniel close to King Nebuchadnezzar. Even though he would refuse to acknowledge God early on, Nebuchadnezzar would eventually realize God's greatness as proclaimed in Daniel 2:47 when he says: *Truly, your God is the greatest of gods, the Lord over kings, a revealer of mysteries, for you have been able to reveal this secret.* Once again, the influence of a godly young man named Daniel had an impact upon an ungodly King to the point that he finally acknowledges the existence and supremacy of God!

So, let me ask you one more time. What will you do if your leader is a loser? If that day should ever come or even if it has already come, I hope you take note of the lessons we learn from Joseph, David and Daniel and apply them to your situations. Remember, God is with you, God is for you, and God is in you...so serve well, my friend!

- **Reflect:** Are you struggling with serving someone who does not embrace or even appreciate your faith?

- **Receive:** Daniel 2:22 says: *God controls the course of world events; He removes kings and sets up other kings.* (NLT)

- **Respond:** Decide today that you will faithfully serve your leader until God releases you, as He might be using you to bring that person to faith in Him.

MY REFLECTIONS

CHAPTER 20

THE PRAYERS OF A SECONDARY LEADER

Confess your sins to each other and pray for each other so that you may be healed. The earnest prayer of a righteous person has great power and produces wonderful results.
(James 5:15)

AS a secondary leader established and purposed by God, your work is cut out for you. Just as the primary leader cannot lead alone, neither can you go it alone. Your strength must flow straight from the Almighty. Your foundation must be on Christ alone. The core of your wisdom must come from God's Word.

With that in mind, as we conclude this work, there are two wonderful scriptures which come together so beautifully and serve as the perfect action call to prayer. The first is found in James 5:16, which says that the fervent prayers of the righteous are powerful and effective. Then we know from 1 John 5:14 that whenever we ask God for something that is within His will, He always hears us.

Man or woman of God, this means when you commit yourself to prayer, not only does God hear you, but your prayers also have a vast and lasting impact. Within God's kingdom you are not a leader in name only...you are an active force, full of the same power that conquered the grave, and commissioned directly by Jesus Christ, our Messiah and King, to go forth and do even greater things than He did. God was not exaggerating when He spoke through the Apostle Paul in Philippians 4:13 that we can do all things through Christ who gives us strength. What does that mean?

It means your prayers change things. It means your prayers advance the cause of Christ in a hurting, dying world. It means your prayers can and do sustain others in powerful ways that you cannot always see.

It is fitting as we conclude this work that we have an action call to prayer. There are several prayers that should be added to the repertoire of each secondary leader, and we will cover them each in turn. I hope you will make these prayers your own. I believe that, over time, you will look back and see how God used your prayers as literal building blocks for His eternal kingdom. What an absolutely incredible thought! It is correct for us to understand that God uses us in unique ways to perfectly accomplish His plans for this world. Each one of us plays a small but vital part within the body of Christ, and therefore God's kingdom is not truly complete without us. A crucial part of our

> When you pray for something within God's will, you in effect are coming into agreement and alignment with God's plans. In doing so, you do not merely "ask God to do something," but rather, you declare that His will be done *on earth as it is in heaven* as Jesus phrased it in Matthew 6:10.

contribution to the kingdom is our prayer life. As a secondary leader, you are ideally positioned to pray for your primary leader as well as for your organization. As a result of your position, you understand the importance of building yourself up in the Lord so you will be all God has divinely purposed for you to be.

These are prayers, yes, but they are so much more than that. They are also declarations. When you pray for something within God's will, you in effect are coming into agreement and alignment with God's plans. In doing so, you do not merely "ask God to do something," but rather, you declare that His will be done *on earth as it is in heaven* as Jesus phrased it in Matthew 6:10. In other words, you are calling forth God's existing plans (that He has already accomplished in the supernatural) to manifest within the natural world.

For example: we do not need to pray weak prayers, begging God to let us make it through another day as if that is the best our omnipotent Father can do. Rather, we declare God's favor on our own lives and that the enemy is defeated. We do not beg God to maybe, just maybe, let someone be saved in the next service; we declare that God's Holy Spirit is welcome in this place, and we invite God to do a mighty work on their behalf. We pray with confidence, knowing God hears us. We declare these things, just as we read in Isaiah 61:1: *The Spirit of the Sovereign Lord is on me, because the Lord has anointed me to proclaim good news to the poor. He has sent me to bind up the brokenhearted, to proclaim freedom for the captives and release from darkness for the prisoners.*

Do you see the difference between praying for God to do something and declaring something that is already within His perfect will? It is always correct to declare God's will! It is always correct to verbally express our agreement with what God already wants to accomplish, even if, at times we do not know any of the details regarding exactly how He will do it. Let us pray and declare with confidence, for God desires nothing less. He will not be offended by your boldness and tenacity; He will smile upon it, for He can see your faith growing and your heart's desire for the kingdom to advance.

With that in mind, there are several areas where each secondary leader can pray. These prayers point you in the right directions in each of these key areas. May God graciously hear and respond in powerful ways as you declare these truths in faith and power!

> Let us pray and declare with confidence, for God desires nothing less.

- **A prayer for your primary leader**

Heavenly Father, I worship You! You alone are the Sovereign Lord, and to You alone will I lift my hands in worship. Lord, my prayer today is for my primary leader. I thank You for the privilege of serving in a leadership capacity, and I thank You for raising up this leader within our organization according to Your own good purposes and perfect will. God, I pray and declare these blessings over him:

- That he will remain firmly rooted in Your love, Your will, and Your Word.

- That he will be rested and refreshed, physically and mentally strengthened for today.

- That he will remember the joy of his calling, marveling anew at Your goodness and love.

- That the flaming arrows of the enemy will be of no effect; that the enemy who attacks him from one direction will promptly flee in terror in seven directions.

- That he will always have a strong and adequate prayer covering, that no spiritual attack against him will linger.

- That his marriage will be strong and complete; that the marriage bed will remain pure; and that the enemy will not in any way be successful in driving a wedge into the marital union which You have ordained.

- That he will be blessed with increased organizational skills, not just to maintain what we already have, but to grow it for the glory of God.

- That You will make available every financial resource needed to fully accomplish the important work You have given to us; and that the hearts of the people will be touched to give, to give generously, and to give extravagantly as You enable them.

- That he will have the favor of both God and man, and that his team will overwhelmingly support him both publicly and privately.

- That the Spirit of unity will be present within the organization as well as in the staff.

- That he will have advisors, friends, and family who come alongside him on this journey. He cannot lead alone, and he cannot feel that he is alone. Remind him that he and his family are dearly loved by so many.

- That he will grow in wisdom, and that he will be powerful in word and in deed.

- That he will be a strong voice of truth in a world filled with deception, and that he will resist the strongest cultural shifts whenever they conflict with the clear message of Christ.

- That he will be led always by the Holy Spirit, never backing down from the truth, faith, hope, healing, and love that You share with him. That no spiritual error will be found in him.

- And that he will give you all glory, all honor, and all praise in everything he does, to the glory of God the Father and Jesus Christ His Son.

In Jesus' mighty Name, amen!

- **A prayer for secondary leaders**

Lord God, You are holy! You are awesome! You are amazing, far beyond my ability to express! I thank You this day that in Your sovereignty, You placed me right where I am, for a specific purpose. My standing as a leader within this organization is no accident, but was divinely appointed according to Your will. I thank You, Heavenly Father, that You are using me to build and advance Your kingdom upon the Earth. I humbly acknowledge that Your plans for me are great, and therefore, I will pray and declare with great faith:

- That You will establish me exactly as You have planned from the foundation of the world, so that Your will might be done.

- That You will grant me increasing wisdom, that I may be prudent in the execution of my duties.

- That I may have favor with You, with my primary leader, and with the other members of my organization to accomplish the work assigned to me.

- That I will publicly and privately support my primary leader, working both visibly and behind the scenes to deliberately promote a spirit of unity. It will never be said of me that I contributed to any disunity. May God be praised!

- That I will support my primary leader in every way through prayer, with finances, and with friendship.

- That I will seek to understand the heavy load my leader shoulders each day, and that I will be an "Aaron and Hur" to help carry that load so every victory you have purposed will come to pass.

- That I will actively look for ways to lighten my leader's load.

- That I will actively encourage my leader, not just during times of stress, but also in good times.

- That You will give me words of wisdom and knowledge, so I know when and how to speak.

- That I will continually invest in the reading of the Word and in bettering myself through spiritual and practical growth.

- That I will not in any way be jealous or envious of the spiritual gifts of others, and that I will not desire any office other than the ones for which You prepare me.

- That the leading of the Holy Spirit will be powerful and evident upon my life.

- That You will grant me the spiritual and practical vision to understand Your purposes for the organization, so that I will remain in alignment with what You seek to accomplish.

- That I will serve with the highest integrity, living as an ambassador for Christ Jesus the Lord of all.

- That I will have both the heart of a leader and the heart of a servant.

- That in all things, let me bring honor to you with all I do, with all I have, and with all I am.

  In Jesus' mighty Name, Amen!

- **A prayer for the local church**

My God and my King, how I love You! How beautiful are Your plans, and how limitless is Your love! You desire great things for Your people, and it is my honor and duty to pray for them. I am humbled that even now You have already answered my prayer that I be planted, established, and rooted exactly where I am, knowing that You have placed me here for a good purpose. I thank you for each member of our congregation. They are made in Your image and in Your likeness, worthy of my genuine love and respect. Therefore, this day I pray and declare these things over them:

- That they will be faithful to You and faithful to our church.

- That their hearts perpetually will be open to the gentle leading of the Holy Spirit.

- That when we assemble as a body of believers, they will desire truth over convenience; worship over entertainment; and spiritual growth over personal comfort.

- That they will be consumed by a hunger for Your Word, not content with the blessings of yesterday but desiring even greater gifts for tomorrow.

- That they will gladly respect the primary leader, honoring him and his family at every opportunity.

- That they will be eager to serve and eager to grow.

- That they will not stand in the way of any move of God, but will resolve to be right in the middle of it for Your glory.

- That You will bless them financially, increasing them so that they may give with increased measure. Let them understand and accept the principle of tithing and bless them wildly for their faithfulness in that area.

- That they will be satisfied with nothing less than a Spirit-filled, Spirit-led church experience.

- That they will be treated with dignity and fairness; and treat others as better than themselves.

- That You will establish them wherever you lead them, in their jobs, their schools, their families, and their neighborhoods.

- That their families will be whole and strong. That mothers and fathers will bring up their children in the Lord. That the children will honor their fathers and mothers, and in doing so, honor You.

- Let their businesses thrive and prosper beyond comprehension.

- Let the enemy be frustrated and confounded by their success; may no evil come near them. May they be protected from the evil one and may no spiritual error take root within their hearts.

- That they will be joyful and glad at the opportunity to go into the house of the Lord!

- That they will be faithful in attendance as you enable them.

- That members of every tongue, tribe, and nation will freely worship within our walls, and that You will tear down and completely destroy every racial and cultural stronghold so that we will worship You with glad and sincere hearts!

- That You will open their minds and understanding to the things You have for our church and for our communities. Let them see how great Your love is and how great are Your plans for them and for our city.

According to Your Word in Hebrews 4:16, I boldly come before the throne of grace with my petition and my request. Hear my prayer and answer from heaven. You alone are the Lord and I pray in Jesus' Name, Amen!

- **Reflect**: Have you ever seen a time when you know with certainty that God answered your prayer?

- **Receive**: 1 John 5:14-15: *And we are confident that he hears us whenever we ask for anything that pleases him. And since we know he hears us when we make our requests, we also know that he will give us what we ask for.*

- **Respond**: Recommit to praying for yourself, your co-workers, your leader, and your organization.

MY REFLECTIONS

REFERENCES

Acknowledgements

[1]Greis, Justin. "Turtles and Fence Posts: Sometimes We all Need a Hand.." https://progressology.com/articles/2014/06/19/turtles-and-fence-posts-sometimes-we-all-need-a-hand/. Accessed May 12, 2022.

Introduction

[1]Sklar, Marty. "Park Perspectives." Disney Files Magazine. Vol. 17, No. 2, Summer 2008. Page 12. https://disneyvacationclub.disney.go.com/media/dvc/languagespecific/eng/member/justformembers/disneyfilesmagazine/2008/DisneyFilesMagazine_Summer2008.pdf. Accessed May 12, 2022.

Chapter 1

[1]"Vince Lombardi Quotes." https://www.goodreads.com/quotes/19425-the-man-on-top-of-the-mountain-didn-t-fall-there. Accessed April 28, 2022.

Chapter 3

[1]Nieuwhof, Carey. "How to Lead Change When You're NOT the Senior Leader." https://careynieuwhof.com/how-to-lead-change-youre-senior-leader/. Accessed April 28, 2022.
[2]Anonymous. "That's When a Man Needs a Brother." https://thelordsway.com/site6/articlesdetail.asp?CongregationID=220&ArticleID=442&return=articles.asp. Accessed April 28, 2022.
[3]Nieuwhof, Carey. "How to Lead Change When You're NOT the Senior Leader." https://careynieuwhof.com/how-to-lead-change-youre-senior-leader/. Accessed April 28, 2022.
[4]Chand, Samuel R with Murphey, Cecil. *Who's Holding Your Ladder?: Selecting Your Leaders, Leadership's Most Critical Decision.* New Kensington, Pennsylvania: Whitaker House, 2016.

Chapter 4

[1]Nieuwhof, Carey. "5 Signs It's Time to Move On." http://careynieuwhof.com/2013/01/5-signs-its-time-to-move-on/. Accessed May 12, 2022.
[2]Rainer, Sam. "Best Follower, The." http://samrainer.com/2014/01/the-best-follower/. Accessed May 12, 2022.

[3]Bonem, Mike. "Fruitful in the Second Chair." http://mikebonem.com/fruitful-in-the-second-chair/. Accessed May 12, 2022.

Chapter 5

[1]Waggoner, Brad. "Leading from the Second Chair." https://churchanswers.com/podcasts/rainer-on-leadership/leading-second-chair-rainer-leadership-072/. Accessed May 12, 2022.
[2]Bonem, Mike. "Is Different Good?" https://mikebonem.com/is-different-good/. Accessed May 12, 2022.
[3]Page, Troy. "Own it!" http://tonymorganlive.com/2014/01/16/own-it/. Accessed May 12, 2022.
[4]Ibid.
[5]Waggoner, Brad. "Leading from the Second Chair." https://churchanswers.com/podcasts/rainer-on-leadership/leading-second-chair-rainer-leadership-072/. Accessed May 12, 2022.

Chapter 6

[1] https://reagan.blogs.archives.gov/2021/01/23/president-reagan-and-the-oval-office/. Accessed May 12, 2022.
[2]Bonem, Mike. "Fruitful in the Second Chair." http://mikebonem.com/fruitful-in-the-second-chair/. Accessed May 12, 2022.
[3]"Five Reasons Second Chair Leaders Should Lift First Chair Leaders." https://www.thehardygroup.org/ArticlesDetail.asp?id=224. Accessed May 12, 2022.

Chapter 8

[1]Waggoner, Brad. "Leading from the Second Chair." https://churchanswers.com/podcasts/rainer-on-leadership/leading-second-chair-rainer-leadership-072/. Accessed July 18, 2022.
[2]Miller, Calvin. *The Empowered Leader – 10 Keys to Servant Leadership.* 1995. Nashville: B&H Publishing Group.
[3]Schwabel, Dan. "Reviving Work Ethic in America." http://www.forbes.com/sites/danschawbel/2011/12/21/reviving-work-ethic-in-america/. Accessed May 12, 2022.
[4]Ibid.

Chapter 9

[1]Smith, Todd. *Speaking in Tongues: Your Secret Weapon.* Dawsonville, Georgia: Independently Published, 2019. Pages 113-114.

Chapter 10
[1]Osbon, Shell. "Boundaries." https://www.lifechurchsmyrna.com/newsite15/wp-content/uploads/2020/09/Boundaries5.pdf Smyrna, Georgia: Life church Smyrna, 2020.
[2]Geiger, Eric. "Peter Principle and the Saul Syndrome, The." http://ericgeiger.com/2015/10/the-peter-principle-and-the-saul-syndrome/#.VhPIJHpViko. Accessed May 12, 2022.

Chapter 12

[1]Dalton, Kyle. "Germ Theory from Antiquity to the Antebellum Period."
https://www.civilwarmed.org/germ-theory-
antebellum/#:~:text=It%20has%20often%20been%20said,humanity%20acknowledged%20t
hem%20or%20not.&text=Disease%20was%20responsible%20for%20two,deaths%20could%2
0have%20been%20prevented. Accessed May 12, 2022.
[2]Stinnett, Bill. "Butterfly Effect, The: Why Small Acts Can Have Big Effects."
https://www.gordontraining.com/leadership/the-butterfly-effect-why-small-acts-can-have-
big-effects. Accessed May 12, 2022.
[3]"Zig Ziglar Quotes." https://quotefancy.com/quote/943730/Zig-Ziglar-It-is-true-that-
integrity-alone-won-t-make-you-a-leader-but-without-integrity. Accessed May 12, 2022.

Chapter 13

[1]Clear, James. "This Coach Improved Every Tiny Thing by 1 Percent and Here's What
Happened." https://jamesclear.com/marginal-gains. Accessed May 12, 2022.

Chapter 14

[1]Kiger, Patrick J. "How Ben Franklin's Viral Political Cartoon United the 13 Colonies."
https://www.history.com/news/ben-franklin-join-or-die-cartoon-french-indian-war.
Accessed May 12, 2022.
[2]Covey, Stephen R. "Stephen R. Covey Quotes."
https://quotefancy.com/quote/909416/Stephen-R-Covey-If-I-were-to-summarize-in-one-
sentence-the-single-most-important. Accessed May 12, 2022.
[3]Cole, Steven J. "Lesson 12: Taming the Terrible Tongue (James 3:1-12).
https://bible.org/seriespage/lesson-12-taming-terrible-tongue-james-31-12. Accessed May
12, 2022.

Chapter 15

[1]Finzel, Hans. *Top Ten Mistakes Leader Make, The*. Wheaton, Illinois: Victor Books, 1994.
p.17.
Lawless, Chuck. "Mentor: How Along-the-Way Discipleship Will Change Your Life."
https://www.lifeway.com/en/product-family/mentor-how-along-the-way-discipleship-will-
change-your-life. Accessed May 12, 2022.

Chapter 16

[1]"Lou Holtz Quotes." https://www.goodreads.com/quotes/28989-never-tell-your-problems-
to-anyone-20-don-t-care-and-the. Accessed May 12, 2022.
[2]"Muhammad Ali Quotes."
https://www.brainyquote.com/quotes/muhammad_ali_148629. Accessed May 12, 2022.

Chapter 17

[1]Engstrom, Ted. *Seizing the Torch*. Ventura, California: Regal Books, 1988.

Chapter 18

[1]Vaughn-Furlow, Becky. "Follow the Leader: Clear Directions Key to Productive Workplace." https://www.clarionledger.com/story/news/2018/05/26/clear-directions-properly-followed-key-productive-workplace/638067002/. Accessed May 12, 2022.

ABOUT THE AUTHOR

SHELL OSBON is the current lead pastor of Life Church Smyrna in Smyrna, Georgia. Since 1986, he has served churches within the Assemblies of God throughout Louisiana and Georgia as a youth pastor, worship leader, business administrator, senior associate pastor, and lead pastor. He has an undergraduate degree in Biblical Education (2003 Summa Cum Laude and Co-Valedictorian) and a Master of Arts degree in Biblical Studies (2009) from Beulah Heights University. He intends to pursue a doctorate degree in the near future.

In addition to his pastoral duties, Shell has been privileged to serve the Georgia Assemblies of God as the Metro Atlanta Regional Presbyter and as an instructor for the Georgia School of Ministry for fifteen years. He previously served as the Alumni Association President and continues to serve as the Vice Chairman of the Board of Trustees for Beulah Heights University. In his community, Shell has served as a board member for SuperSmyrna, First Priority Ministries, the City of Smyrna's Ten-Year Vision for the Community and the Smyrna Citizen Corp Council. He currently serves on the Griffin Middle School Counselor Advisory Committee, and as a Chaplain for the Smyrna Fire Department, Smyrna Police Department, City of Smyrna employees, and the Smyrna Business Association. He is also a board member for the Smyrna Public Safety Foundation and Spiritual Adviser for the Code 7 Foundation.

Shell has been married to his wife, Missy, since 1986. They reside in Austell, Georgia. Their son, S.J., his wife, Tina, and their three children live in Smyrna, Georgia, while their daughter, Summer Joy, her husband Gary, and their two children live in Hiram, Georgia.

For more information on the work and ministry of Shell Osbon, visit the Life Church Smyrna website at:

www.lifechurchsmyrna.com

PRAISE FOR *IT'S NOT GOOD FOR LEADERS TO LEAD ALONE:*

"Yes, you can do it all. But not much. Shell Osbon establishes that vigorously in *It's NOT Good for Leaders to Lead Alone!*" Regardless of where you are positionally in your organization you will find this book helpful, inspirational, and pragmatic. I would encourage all leaders at all levels to read and share the message of this important book." (Dr. Sam Chand, Leadership Consultant and Author of *Ladder Leaders,* samchand.com)

"Thought-provoking and powerful! Pastor Shell Osbon passionately stated what it means to be a leader. He masterfully demonstrated what leadership means." (Dr. Benson Karanja, President of Beulah Heights University, beulah.org)

"Every quarterback needs a good receiver to catch the ball in hopes to score the winning touchdown. And after a being a Pastor for over forty years, it is imperative to have the right team and the right blueprint for successful leadership. In this great book, Shell Osbon pens a masterful guide that will surely help any leader be intentional about purposeful leadership. This book makes a compelling case for the kind of leadership we need today." (Bishop Paul S. Morton, Sr., Founder of the Full Gospel Baptist Church Fellowship International; Senior Pastor of Changing a Generation Ministries, Atlanta, GA; Overseer and Co-Pastor of Greater St. Stephen Ministries, New Orleans, LA; CAGNOW.org)

"Abraham needed Isaac and Jacob to found Israel. Moses needed Joshua. Elijah needed Elisha. David needed Solomon. Paul needed Barnabas, Silas, and finally Mark. Even Jesus needed a team of disciples. Every leader needs team mates. Shell Osbon looks at the benefits of teaming from the alpha leader's point of view as well as the view of those following. He provides wisdom and applicable strategies for answering problems and troublesome questions. While reading this valuable manuscript you will become grateful for your place on the team and more appreciative of those following you, going with you, and leading you. You will be better, and you will never want to try to lead alone again!" (Dr. Terry Raburn, Superintendent, Peninsular Florida Assemblies of God, penflorida.org)

"Shell Osbon has captured in the book what the heart of God is towards leadership (mainly in but not limited to the pastoral context). Good leaders function effectively in plurality with other leaders who are singularly aligned in purpose, mission, heart, and philosophy. Unlike most books on leadership, Osbon does a lot more heavy lifting by actually exploring how secondary leaders should serve rather than just talking about qualities and characteristics of leadership. I highly recommend this book to pastors at every level, who are desiring to develop themselves and others in Christ-centered leadership." (Dr. Damon Richardson, Founder of UrbanLogia Ministries, urbanlogia.org)

"Leadership doesn't mean that you have to be the single point of influence for an organization. It means building a team and encouraging members to lead from wherever you are. Pastor Shell is right on target with his book, and encouraging readers to lead from their position, towards the vision and successes established for us by Jesus Christ. I highly recommend this book and reaching out to Pastor Shell. He is moving the Church forward." (Brigadier General Stewart Rodeheaver, US Army [Ret.], President of ViziTech USA, vizitechusa.com)

"Leadership is about walking together for God and the good of humanity. Pastor's new book is a call to everyone, and most specifically, secondary leaders to be content in their God-given assignment and die to ambition and ego. This book will be a great tool in the years ahead as secondary leaders also learn to be close followers of Jesus in their daily work. You will want to give this book to your team and see the impact it has on your organization." (Dr. Mike Rakes, Lead Pastor of Winston-Salem First, wsfirst.com)

"Pastor Shell Osbon has written this book primarily for the secondary leader; however, its content reminds the primary leader how he or she got on the fence post. This book is a must read for every leader whether primary or secondary. The book is an excellent staff development curriculum so that the primary and secondary leaders work together to advance the organization." (Bishop Jerry Hutchins, Founding Pastor of Kingdom Now Ministries, kingdom-now.org)

"I have studied leadership theory for many years and as a public servant, it was my aspiration to be a servant leader with transformational vision. No one embraces that philosophy better than Pastor Shell Osbon in his powerful rendition of the importance of leadership. A primary leader

must allow and encourage the ability for secondary leaders to have the empowerment to "grow" the organization forward. *It is Not Good for Leaders to Lead Alone* offers introspective questions that the reader has the opportunity to not only ponder how this applies to their leadership style, but also challenge themselves to better support the organizational mission."
(Paige Day, Ed.D. [abd.], Fire Chief (ret.), Director of Hydronalix, hydronalix.com)

"Shell Osbon has invested his years of personal and ministerial experience in creating a valuable, critical, and practical roadmap for current and future leaders. Whether as a primary leader or supporter from the second chair, before you say yes to the assignment, take time to read this book. You will be better equipped to both pass and receive the baton of leadership." Dr. D'Ann V. Johnson, Executive Pastor of New Covenant Christian Ministries (newcov.org), Author and Founder of Overflow Ministries International, liveintheoverflow.org):

"Throughout this book Pastor Osbon reminds us that we are all called to a specific place for a specific time to serve the greater good, and as leaders, we can't do that alone!" (Dr. Cindy Szwec, King Springs Elementary School Principal, cobbk12.org/KingSprings)

"Leadership is a complex and nuanced undertaking, even for the most stalwart personalities among us. 'Second-tier leadership' in particular tests the tensile strength of one's love and loyalty daily, calling upon reserves of creativity, humility, and courage. In his new book, *It's Not Good for Leaders to Lead Alone*, Pastor Shell Osbon interrogates the leadership enterprise, posing critical questions that leaders at every level must answer. I encourage you to read it to become a more skilled and faithful leader." (Dr. Johnathan Alvarado, Senior Pastor of Grace Church International, gracechurchintl.org)

"First, I will say, the person reading this book will, whether a primary or secondary leader, learn from the heart of a man who lives the life described here. Pastor Shell writes with a sense of purpose, adds humor, and offers wisdom that comes only from walking through life experiencing the opportunities and observing the Spirit of God's manifestations come alive. Every staff member, leader, and volunteer in every church should have this book in their hands. The lessons will prove invaluable." (Reverend Paul Steeger, Outreach/Missions Director of Abundant Life Church, abundantlifechurch.us; Chaplain for Maryland Capitol Police, mcp.maryland.gov)

"One of the greatest leadership hacks comes from the father-in-law of Moses in saying, 'You and the people with you will certainly wear yourselves out, for the thing is too heavy for you. You are not able to do it alone.' No leader should lead alone and, in this book, Pastor Osbon masterfully unites leaders and teams with practical steps to ensure that the team is equipped to work well in order to make the dream work." (Bishop Kevin Foreman, Pastor of Harvest Church, Chancellor of Harvest Bible College, President of the Harvest Leadership Network, bishopforeman.com)

"I must admit when I started reading this book, *It's Not Good for Leaders to Lead Alone*, I was caught off guard. I assumed that it was going to exhort me as a Lead Pastor to develop other leaders to partner with me. But, to my surprise and delight, Shell Osbon has given all of us a gift in affirming the role, responsibilities, and rewards of being a staff member serving a Lead Pastor. This is a must-read for all those who serve in a secondary position and want to be happy and fulfilled in it." (Dr. Cynthia L. Hale, Lead Pastor of Ray of Hope Christian Church, rayofhope.org)

"Leadership context, in today's literary world, is primarily addressed to define and instruct 'primary' leaders. In this book, Shell Osbon addresses 'secondary' leaders to help shape and clarify the nature of their calling by creating cultures of honor as they serve their 'primary' leaders in the work of the local church and beyond. I'm certain that this book will bless and strengthen the work of our hands!" (Dr. Mark Merrill, Former Superintendent, GA Assemblies of God, gadistag.org)

Made in the USA
Columbia, SC
03 August 2022

64531278R00104